Wood Pellet Smoker and Grill Cookbook

The Ultimate Wood Pellet Smoker and Grill Cookbook – The Ultimate Guide and Recipe Book for the Most Delicious and Flavorful Barbecue

Table of Contents

Introduction

I want to thank you for choosing this book, 'Wood Pellet Smoker and Grill Cookbook: The Ultimate Wood Pellet Smoker and Grill Cookbook – The Ultimate Guide and Recipe Book for The Most Delicious and Flavorful Barbecue.'

Who doesn't love barbecue! It is an all-American tradition that has been popular since time immemorial. Once considered to be the only means for traditional southern tribes to cook their food, barbecuing slowly transitioned into a family tradition.

Right from children to grandparents, everybody loves to take part in barbecue parties and sink their teeth into smoked, grilled delicious food. But as exciting as it sounds, traditional coal barbecue machines can be a pain to setup, use and clean. Not to mention the thick smoke they create, they can smoke out the entire room!

This prompted an inventor in 1982 to experiment with wooden pellets that could replace the coal, and make it easier for people to smoke and grill. Thus came about a wood pellet smoker and grill. The machine is simple to use and helps you make some of the tastiest and delicious barbecues. You do not have to worry about the fuss that a traditional barbecue creates and can focus on the cooking.

This book will serve as your ultimate wood pellet smoker and grill cookbook and take you through multiple, delicious recipes that you can cook using your wood pellet smoker grill.

The recipes are all easy to put together and can be made by just about anyone!

Let us begin!

Chapter 1: What is a Wood Pellet Smoker-Grill?

In this chapter, we will look at a wood pellet smoker grill in detail. A wood pellet smoker grill is a barbecue machine that makes use of wood pellets instead of coal. This makes it easier to use, clean up and it also produces a woody flavor.

Mechanism

The wood pellet smoker grill is unlike a traditional barbecue, which makes use of coal as the fuel. Wood pellets are pellets made from compressed sawdust and wood shavings. They are put into a hopper and then added to a burn pot that uses an electric auger system.

The auger is nothing but a long screw that moves the pellets to the burn pot. This movement can be controlled using the thermostat.

As and when the burn pot ignites, the pellets start to burn. The heat is then carried to the grill through air vents thereby incorporating air into the process. This ensures that both warm and cool air passes through thereby maintaining a consistent temperature.

This prevents burning and ensures that food is cooked evenly. A heat exchanger helps in separating the smoke from the hot air thereby controlling the smoke from spreading throughout the room.

The entire machine runs on electricity thus making it ideal for all households. You can now forget about having to blow into the coal furnace to light it up.

Wood pellet smoker grills come with a catch plate under the machine that catches all the drips. This means that it is much easier for you to clean up and treat yourself to a healthier meal.

Using the wood pellet smoker grill

It is incredibly easy to use the wood pellet smoker grill. You must start off by heating up the machine. Flip the switch to move the pellets to the hopper. You can then set your ideal temperature and wait for the pellets to start glowing and burning.

Is it a grill or a smoker?

The wood pellet smoker and grill serves as both a grill and a smoker. Once it is ready, you can start grilling and smoking your meat.

Chapter 2: Why Use a Wood Pellet Smoker-Grill? Advantages/Disadvantages

A wood pellet smoker grill is a handy machine that can be used to replace a traditional barbecue machine. It makes for a better choice owing to different reasons, and they are as follows.

Advantages of using wood pellet smoker grill

Flavor

One of the biggest benefits of using a wood pellet smoker grill is the woody flavor that it lends to dishes. You can choose from a variety of woods such as apple, hardwood, cedar, maple, etc. All of these give a unique flavor to the meats and make them taste amazing.

Smoke

Wood pellet smoker grills do not produce a lot of smoke and will not force you to carry out barbecuing outside your house. You can set it up right in the comfort of your home and start barbecuing. The machine will also not smoke out your meat too much. It will be a subtle flavor and not too smoky.

Temperatures

You can choose from a wide temperature range and set the oven to a temperature of your choice. This makes it easier for you to cook your meats at the right temperature. You don't have to worry about over cooking or undercooking it and be sure of perfectly cooked meat every time.

Ease of use

Wood pellet smokers and grills are incredibly easy to use and can be utilized by just about anyone. You can switch it on, pick the ideal temperature and carry on with other chores. It is ideal when entertaining family and friends as you can engage with them instead of standing by the smoker grill.

Consistency

Wood pellet ovens give you incredible consistency and results. They work well with all types of meats and cook evenly on all sides. You don't have to worry about tossing and turning food now and then, as the oven will evenly cook the meat.

Uses

The smoker grill can be used to serve a variety of uses including grilling, smoking, braising, roasting, etc. One machine alone will carry out all of these tasks thereby making it easy for you to cook elaborate meals.

Disadvantages of a wood pellet smoker grill

There are a few disadvantages to using a wood pellet smoker grill, and they are as follows:

Mobility

As you know, wood pellet smoker grills run on electricity and thus will require an electric source. This means you will not be able to take it out to picnics unless you carry a generator along.

Sears

Wood pellet smoker grills will not create searing marks that you would expect with barbecued foods. This might be a little disappointing for some people, as they would expect to have the grill marks on their meats.

Smoke

Although the machine tries to control the smoke to a large extent, it might not be able to control it fully. If you are grilling at a low temperature, then it can produce a lot of smoke.

Chapter 3: History of Wood Pellet Smoker-Grill

Wood pellet smoker grills date back to 1980s. Traeger Pellet Grills are said to have been the first company to offer wood pellet smoker grills to the market.

The founder, Joe Traeger, made use of wood pellets as fuel for a barbecue smoker that he came up with as an alternate use of the home heating furnace that he was selling. With time, a thermostat was added in thereby incorporating the feature of set it and forget it. Since then, several companies set up their businesses and slowly began to introduce wood pellet smoker grills.

There are now many models to choose from, and you can pick one that suits your needs.

Chapter 4: Poultry Recipes Using a Wood Pellet-Smoker Grill

Smoked Chicken with Apricot Glaze

Ingredients:

- 2 whole chicken, trimmed and halved
- 4 tablespoons chicken rub
- 1 cup apricot barbecue sauce

Instructions:

1. Start off by preparing the smoker grill. To do so, switch it on and keep the lid open. Wait for a fire to establish.
2. Set the temperature to 375 F.
3. Keep the lid closed for 10 to 15 minutes.
4. Meanwhile, add the chicken and rub to a bowl and mix until well combined.
5. Add to the oven and cook for an hour until the internal temperature reaches 160 degrees in the breast area and 175 degrees in the leg area.
6. Baste the chicken with the barbecue sauce and return to the grill.
7. Grill for 10 minutes.
8. Remove from grill and allow it to rest for 5 to 10 minutes.
9. Gently separate the legs and breast pieces to remain with 4 legs and 8 breast pieces.
10. Serve the chicken with vegetables of your choice.

Smoked Chicken Sandwich

Ingredients:

- 4 boneless chicken breasts
- ¾ cup vinegar
- ½ cup ricotta cheese
- ½ tablespoon parsley leaves

For brine

- ¼ cup salt
- ¼ cup brown sugar

For cheese spread

- ½ tablespoon chives, chopped
- 1 teaspoon lemon zest
- ¼ cup chicken rub
- 2 cups rice
- 1 cup cherries
- Orange zest
- Salt and pepper to taste

Instructions:

1. Add the salt and sugar to a bowl and toss in the chicken.
2. Do this 2 to 3 days in advance and allow it to stay in the brine.
3. Place the grill on smoke with the top open until it fires up.
4. Set the temperature to 275 F and preheat for 10 to 15 minutes.
5. Remove the chicken from brine and pat dry. Place the chicken on the grill and cook for 2 hours. The internal temperature has to reach 165 F.
6. Meanwhile, mix together the vinegar, sugar, salt, pepper and orange zest and add to a saucepan until dissolved.
7. Pour it all over the cherries and place in the fridge.
8. Mix together the cheese, parsley, chives, lemon zest, salt and pepper.

WOOD PELLET SMOKER AND GRILL COOKBOOK

9. Once the chicken is done, allow it to cool down before slicing.
10. To make the sandwich, spread the mustard on one side of the bread and the cheese spread on the other.
11. Add the sliced chicken, cherries and arugula and close the sandwich and serve.

Citrus Turkey

Ingredients:

- 15 pounds turkey
- 3 tablespoon salt
- 1 tablespoon garlic
- 1 tablespoon onion powder
- 3 tablespoons Italian seasoning
- 4 oranges
- 2 lemons
- Cilantro leaves
- Butter spray
- Chicken seasoning

Instructions:

1. Mix the garlic, onion powder and Italian seasoning to make a dry rub.
2. Add in the turkey and rub it in.
3. Do this 3 days in advance in order to make brine.
4. Start the smoker grill and allow it to heat up.
5. Once done, place the turkey on the grill and layer the oranges, lemons, and herbs.
6. Cook it at 275 F for 3 to 4 hours.
7. The turkey has to reach an internal temperature of 165 F.
8. Slice it warm and serve.

Chicken Bacon Skewers

Ingredients:

- ½ cup ranch dressing
- 3 tablespoons barbecue rub
- 1 tablespoon hot sauce
- 4 chicken breasts, skinned and boned
- 20 red onions, quartered
- 10 slices thick cut bacon
- 10 to 12 skewers

Instructions:

1. Add the ranch dressing to a bowl along with the hot sauce and rub and mix together until well combined.
2. Remove ⅓ of the mix for later use.
3. Add the chicken to the mix in the bowl and rub well.
4. Cover it and place in the fridge for 1 to 3 hours.
5. Preheat the grill to 275 F.
6. Remove the chicken from the sauce and discard it.
7. Pat it dry using papers.
8. Slowly skewer the chicken pieces onto the skewer and alternate between onions and bacon.
9. Aim at having 5 to 6 pieces of chicken per skewer.
10. Secure them by placing onions on the open side.
11. Cook the skewers by turning them every 6 to 8 minutes.
12. Make sure they brown on each and every side.
13. Serve hot.

BBQ Chicken Thighs

Ingredients:

- 6 chicken thighs, bone in
- 1 bottle chicken rub
- Salt and pepper to taste

Instructions:

1. Open the lid of the grill and allow the fire to establish.
2. Set the temperature to 350 F.
3. Keep the lid closed for 10 to 15 minutes.
4. In the meantime, trim the chicken down.
5. Sprinkle salt and pepper on top and rub it in.
6. Spread the game rub all over it.
7. Place the chicken on the grill and grill for 35 minutes.
8. The internal temperature should reach 165 F.
9. Remove from the grill and let it cool down for 5 to 10 minutes.
10. Serve hot.

Duck Breast

Ingredients:

- 4 duck breasts
- Salt to taste
- Pepper to taste

Instructions:

1. Add the duck breasts to a plate and pat dry.
2. Use a sharp knife to make incisions over the duck breast.
3. But be careful not to cut into the meat.
4. Allow it to stay at room temperature for 30 minutes.
5. Open the lid of the smoker grill and let the fire establish.
6. Set the temperature to high and keep for 10 to 15 minutes.
7. Sprinkle the salt and pepper over the duck breasts and rub it in.
8. Place the breasts on the skillet and press down.
9. Close the lid.
10. Check on the duck after 15 to 20 minutes and check the skin.
11. It has to turn golden brown.
12. This might take about 5 to 10 minutes.
13. Once the skin crisps up flip it over.
14. Cook for a further 5 to 10 minutes.
15. The internal temperature of the meat should reach 130 to 135 F.
16. Let it cool on a cutting board for 5 to 10 minutes before carving.

Portuguese Chicken

Ingredients:

- 1 whole chicken
- ½ cup lemon juice
- 2 tablespoons sugar
- 4 garlic cloves
- 1 red chili
- Salt to taste
- 3 tablespoons sweet paprika
- 2 tablespoons dried oregano

Instructions:

1. Add the lemon juice, oil, paprika, sugar, garlic, red chili and salt to a bowl and mix until combined.
2. Add the chicken in and rub well.
3. Add to the fridge for 24 hours.
4. Open the lid of the grill and allow it to heat up.
5. Set the temperature to 350 F.
6. Close the lid for 10 to 15 minutes.
7. Add the chicken to the grill and roast until the internal temperature reaches 165 F.
8. Take it out and let it rest for 15 to 20 minutes before carving and serving.

Maple Brine Turkey

Ingredients:

- 1 large turkey
- 5 quarts water
- 2 tablespoons peppercorns
- 1 tablespoon cloves
- ½ cup salt
- 1 cup maple syrup
- 1 large onion, peeled and chopped
- 3 bay leaves
- Poultry shake
- Thyme, rosemary

Instructions:

1. Add the salt, water, bourbon, maple syrup, brown sugar, onions, bay leaves, orange peel, peppercorns and cloves to a container and mix until well combined.
2. Clean the turkey thoroughly before adding to the brine.
3. Add to the fridge for 8 to 12 hours.
4. Drain and pat dry the turkey.
5. Discard the brine and tie the back legs together.
6. Mix the butter and maple syrup together.
7. Apply it over the turkey using a pastry brush.
8. Sprinkle the salt; pepper and poultry rub over the turkey.
9. Open the lid of the grill and allow a fire to establish.
10. Set the temperature to 350 F.
11. Close the lid for 10 to 15 minutes.
12. Roast the turkey for 2 to 3 hours or till the internal temperature reaches 165 F.
13. Remove the turkey out and allow it to cool down for 15 to 20 minutes.
14. Carve and serve.

Seared Duck Breasts

Ingredients:

- 3 ounces game rub
- 3 duck breasts

Instructions:

1. Open the lid of the grill and allow a fire to establish.
2. Set the temperature to high or 500 F.
3. Close the lid and heat for 10 to 15 minutes.
4. Meanwhile, season the duck breasts using the rub and gently score over the surface of the skin.
5. Allow the duck to rest for 10 to 15 minutes.
6. Add to the grill and sear on both sides.
7. Flip it every 4 to 5 minutes.
8. Allow it to cool for 10 minutes before carving and serving.

Spatchcock Roast

Ingredients:

- 4 game hens
- 2 ounces game rub

Instructions:

1. Place the hens on the cutting board and use sharp shears to cut into the tailbone and neck.
2. Gently remove the backbone to reveal the inside of the bird.
3. Make small incisions in the bird.
4. Split the bird open like a book.
5. Season both the sides of the bird with the rub.
6. Open the lid of the grill and allow a fire to establish.
7. Set the temperature to 275 F and close the lid for 10 to 15 minutes.
8. Place the bird's skin side up on the grill and cook until the internal temperature reaches 160 F.
9. Add to a cutting board and let it rest for 10 minutes.
10. Carve and serve.

Spicy Chicken

Ingredients:

- 1 whole chicken
- 5 chilies
- 2 tablespoons paprika
- Salt to taste
- 1 large onion
- 5 garlic cloves
- 4 cups oil
- 2 tablespoons sugar
- 1 scotch bonnet pepper

Instructions:

1. Add the chilies, paprika, pepper, sugar, salt, onion, garlic and oil to a blender and whizz until smooth and add to a bowl.
2. Add the chicken to the mix and marinate for 10 minutes.
3. Open the lid of the machine and allow a fire to establish.
4. Set the temperature to 300 F.
5. Let it sit for 10 minutes.
6. Add the chicken to the grill for 3 hours or until the internal temperature reaches 165 F.
7. Allow it to cool down before slicing and serving.

Baked Turkey Pie

Ingredients:

- 3 cups peas and carrots, frozen
- 2 cups broccoli, chopped
- 3 cups chicken stock
- 1 cup milk
- Salt to taste
- 1 tablespoon thyme, chopped
- 1 tablespoon rosemary, chopped
- ⅛ cup cornstarch
- Salt to taste
- Pepper to taste
- 3 tablespoons butter
- 3 cups wild turkey, preferably left over
- 1 sheet puff pastry

Instructions:

1. Keep the lid of the grill open until a fire establishes.
2. Set the temperature to 375 F and close the lid for 10 to 15 minutes.
3. In the meantime add the chicken stock, milk, butter and herbs to a pot.
4. Bring it to a boil.
5. Add the cornstarch and little water to a bowl and mix well.
6. Once it boils add the cornstarch and stir well.
7. Add the salt and pepper and combine.
8. Add the peas, carrots, broccoli and turkey to a bowl and mix.
9. Add the sauce to the mix.
10. Add it to a baking dish or iron skillet.
11. Cover it with the puff pastry and trim the edges.
12. Apply the butter on top.
13. Place it on the grill and cook for an hour and 20 minutes.
14. Remove it from the grill and allow to rest for 10 to 15 minutes.
15. Slice and serve.

Chicken Chili

Ingredients:

- 4 chicken thighs, boneless
- 3 cups chicken broth
- 3 cups salsa verde
- 1 cup onion, chopped
- 2 teaspoon cumin seeds, powdered
- Olive oil
- 1 tablespoon garlic, chopped
- 1 cup corn kernels
- 1 teaspoon oregano
- ½ teaspoon cumin seeds
- Salt to taste
- Pepper to taste

Instructions:

1. Open the lid of the smoker grill and allow the fire to establish.
2. Set the temperature to 350 F.
3. Add the chicken to a bowl and toss with the onions, salt, and pepper.
4. Add the chicken to the grill and grill until cooked on both sides.
5. Meanwhile, add a skillet over the grill and add in the oil.
6. Add the onions, garlic, cumin, corn, oregano, and sauté.
7. Add the salsa, chicken broth and cover to cook for 10 minutes.
8. Chop the chicken thighs and add to the sauce and sauté.
9. Serve hot.

Chicken Tostadas

Ingredients:

- 4 boneless chicken thighs
- 10 corn tostadas
- Refried beans
- Lettuce leaves, sliced
- Green onion, chopped
- Guacamole
- Cilantro chopped

Instructions:

1. Open the lid and wait for a fire to establish.
2. Set the temperature to 350 F and set for 10 minutes.
3. Meanwhile, trim the excess fat from the meat and season with salt and pepper.
4. Place the thighs on the grill for 35 minutes.
5. The internal temperature has to reach 175 F.
6. Remove from the grill and let it rest for some time.
7. In the meantime, place the tostadas on the grill for 5 minutes.
8. Make it to your liking by adding in the beans, lettuce, chicken, tomatoes, onions and guacamole and serve.

Beer Chicken

Ingredients:

- 2 tablespoons olive oil
- 2 tablespoons chicken rub
- ¼ cup all-purpose flour
- Salt to taste
- 3 pounds chicken
- 1 large onion, chopped
- 2 garlic cloves, chopped
- 2 carrots, chopped
- 1 red pepper, chopped
- 1 can tomatoes
- 10 ounces beer
- 10 small potatoes

Instructions:

1. Open the lid of the grill and allow the fire to establish.
2. Keep the lid closed for 10 to 15 minutes and set the temperature to 350.
3. Place a Dutch oven on the smoker and grill.
4. Add the flour, salt, chicken rub and pepper to a bowl and mix well.
5. Heat the oil in the Dutch oven and add in the chicken pieces.
6. Allow it to cook on both sides or until golden brown.
7. Remove the chicken and let it rest.
8. Add the onions, garlic, and pepper to the oil and sauté.
9. Add in the carrots and sauté.
10. Add the tomatoes and combine.
11. Toss in the salt and let it cook for 5 minutes.
12. Add the chicken pieces to the top of the stew.
13. Serve warm.

Smoked Chicken with Jalapeno Sauce

Ingredients:

- 8 chicken pieces, quartered
- 2 tablespoons salt
- ¼ cup sugar
- Red chili, chopped
- 2 tablespoons paprika
- 1 tablespoon garlic, chopped
- 1 onion, chopped
- 1 tablespoon coriander seeds, crushed
- 1 tablespoon pepper
- 1 tablespoon cumin seeds
- 1 teaspoon fennel seeds
- Salt to taste
- Pepper to taste
- Olive oil

Instructions:

1. Add the paprika, garlic, onion, and coriander seeds to a bowl and add the chicken to it.
2. Use your hands to massage the chicken carefully.
3. Set it aside for 3 to 6 hours or overnight.
4. To make the sauce, cut open the jalapeno and remove the seeds.
5. Add it to a blender along with the oil, salt and pepper and whizz until smooth.
6. Toss in the cilantro and parsley and whizz further.
7. When the mixer is running, add in the oil and lemon and keep whizzing.
8. Open the lid and allow a fire to establish.
9. Set the temperature to 225 F and close the lid for 10 minutes.
10. Add the chicken to the grill and close it for 2 hours.
11. The internal temperature should reach 165 F.
12. Remove and let it rest for 10 minutes.
13. Pour the jalapeno sauce over it and serve.

Asian Chicken Wings

Ingredients:

- 3 pounds chicken
- 2 tablespoons garlic, chopped
- ¼ cup shallots
- ½ inch ginger
- ½ cup lemongrass
- 3 tablespoons sugar
- 1/4 cup fish sauce
- 3 tablespoons lime juice
- 3 tablespoons peanut oil
- Salt to taste
- ¼ cup roasted peanuts
- ¼ cup cilantro leaves, chopped

Instructions:

1. Rinse the wings thoroughly and pat it dry.
2. Add the garlic, shallots, ginger, sugar, scallions, lemongrass, fish sauce, lime juice and peanut oil into a blender and whizz until smooth.
3. Add the chicken to the marinade and massage it in.
4. Open the lid of the grill and allow a fire to establish.
5. Set the temperature to 350 F and close the lid for 10 minutes.
6. Add the chicken pieces to the grill and grill on both sides.
7. This can take 30 to 50 minutes.
8. Remove to a platter, cut and serve.

BBQ Turkey

Ingredients:

- 6 thighs, bone in
- 1 bottle game rub of your choice
- Salt to taste
- Pepper to taste

Instructions:

1. Open the lid and allow a fire to establish.
2. Set the temperature to 350 F and close lid for 10 minutes.
3. Remove the fat and from the turkey and add to a bowl along with the salt and pepper.
4. Place the thighs on the grill for 35 minutes or until the outside is crispy.
5. The internal temperature should reach 165 F.
6. Remove and allow to rest for 5 minutes.
7. Serve hot.

Turkey Wraps

Ingredients:

- 1 large boneless turkey breast
- 1 bottle game rub
- Bread to wrap

Instructions:

1. Open the lid and wait for a fire to establish.
2. Set the temperature to 325 F and close the lid for 10 minutes.
3. Add the turkey to a bowl and toss in the rub.
4. Place the turkey on the grill and
5. The internal temperature should reach 165 F.
6. Allow it to cool, slice and add to a wrap.
7. Serve warm.

Sausage Rolls

Ingredients:

- 1 pound chicken mince
- 1 cup bread crumbs
- 1 egg, beaten
- 1 medium zucchini, grated
- 1 white onion, chopped
- 1 medium carrot, chopped
- ½ cup flat-leaf parsley leaves, chopped
- 1 teaspoon dried thyme leaves
- 1 teaspoon garlic, chopped
- ¼ cup Thai chili sauce
- 4 sheets puff pastry
- 1 egg, beaten
- 1 teaspoon sesame seeds

Instructions:

1. Add the chicken, eggs, breadcrumbs, zucchini, onion and carrot to a bowl and mix well.
2. Place a pastry sheet on a floured working board and add 2 tablespoons of the mix in the center.
3. Fold an open end of the pastry dough to cover the filling.
4. Fold over the remaining side to make a tight parcel.
5. Open the lid and allow a fire to establish.
6. Set the temperature to 375 F and close the lid for 15 minutes.
7. Add the eggs to a bowl and beat.
8. Add the parcels to the grill and close the lid.
9. Cook for 30 minutes.
10. Serve warm.

Thanksgiving Turkey

Ingredients:

- 1 whole turkey
- 2 sticks of butter
- 1 celery stalk, chopped
- 1 carrot, chopped
- 1 cup chicken broth
- 1 onion, chopped
- 2 tablespoons parsley, chopped
- 2 tablespoons rosemary, chopped
- 2 tablespoons sage, chopped
- 2 tablespoons thyme, chopped
- 1 orange zest
- Salt to taste
- Pepper to taste

Instructions:

1. Tuck the turkey tail under the turkey and tie the drumsticks together.
2. Open the lid and allow a fire to establish.
3. Set the temperature to 375 F and close the lid for 15 minutes.
4. Add the carrots, celery, onion, parsley, rosemary, sage, thyme, orange zest, salt and pepper to a bowl and mix well.
5. Add it inside the cavity of the chicken.
6. Tie the legs of the chicken using cooking thread.
7. Add the chicken to a tray and pour the chicken broth over it.
8. Add the tray to the smoker grill and close the lid.
9. Cook for 40 minutes or until the internal temperature reaches 165 F.
10. Take the turkey out and let it cool for 10 minutes before carving and serving.

Chapter 5: Red Meat Recipes Using a Wood Pellet-Smoker Grill

Grilled Beef Burger

Ingredients:

- 1 pound beef mince
- Salt to taste
- Pepper to taste
- 2 onions, chopped
- 4 to 5 burger buns
- 4 to 5 slices cheese

Instructions:

1. Add the beef, salt, and pepper to a bowl and mix until well combined.
2. Make about 5 balls out of the mix.
3. Open the lid of the smoker grill and allow a fire to establish.
4. Place a griddle on the grill and wait for it to heat up for 15 minutes.
5. Once done, add a little oil and use a brush to spread it.
6. Add one ball on the griddle and smash it using a spatula.
7. Add about half of the onions on the patties.
8. Carefully flip the buns over and make sure the onions remain on top.
9. Add the buns to the griddle.
10. Once they soften, add the buns in between and add the rest of the onions.
11. Add the cheese slices on top.
12. Close and serve.

Steak with Green Onions

Ingredients:

- 2 large steaks
- Salt to taste
- Pepper to taste
- 2 pounds mixed greens
- 2 tablespoons butter
- 2 garlic pods, crushed
- 1 large shallot, chopped
- 1 cup heavy cream
- 1 teaspoon all spice powder

Instructions:

1. Open the lid of the smoker grill and allow a fire to establish.
2. Set the temperature to 350 F and close the lid for 10 minutes.
3. Add the steak to a plate and add the salt and pepper to it.
4. Add the steaks to the grill and close for 45 minutes.
5. The internal temperature should reach 120 F.
6. Remove the steaks and close the lid for 10 minutes.
7. Add the steak back to the grill for 15 minutes or until the internal temperature reaches 130 F.
8. To make the greens, add the butter to a pan placed over the grill and allow it to heat up.
9. Toss in the garlic and shallot and sauté until golden.
10. Add in the cream to it and stir for 10 minutes.
11. Add in the all spice to it and mix well.
12. Add this to a blender to make a smooth paste or use a hand blender to do so.
13. Add in salt and mix well.
14. Add the steak to a plate and spread the sauce on top.

Short Ribs

Ingredients:

- 4 short ribs
- 1 bottle rib rub

Instructions:

1. Thoroughly clean the ribs and add them to a plate.
2. Open the lid of the grill and allow a fire to establish.
3. Set the temperature to 250 F and close the lid for 15 minutes.
4. Add the ribs to the grill and close the lid.
5. The internal temperature of the beef should reach about 160 F.
6. Spread aluminum foil on the table and add the steaks on top.
7. Fold the foil from the sides and pack firmly leaving one end open.
8. Add the ribs back to the grill and allow it to reach 204 F.
9. Remove and wait for the ribs to cool for 10 minutes.
10. Slice and serve.

Juicy Burgers

Ingredients:

- 1 pound beef mince
- Salt to taste
- Pepper to taste
- 5 burger buns
- Pickles of your choice
- Cheese slices

Instructions:

1. Tear the cheese slices into 4 and stack them on a plate.
2. Add the beef mince, salt and pepper to a bowl and mix until well combined.
3. Make 5 balls out of the mix and add to a working surface.
4. Flatten the patties and make a dent in the center by pressing down using your thumb.
5. Add a stack of the cheese and fold the meat over it.
6. Make a ball out of it and then press it down again.
7. Open the lid of the grill and allow a fire to establish.
8. Set the temperature to 400 F and close the lid for 10 minutes.
9. Place the burger patties on the grill followed by the buns.
10. The internal temperature of the patties should reach 140 F.
11. Add the patties to the center of the buns and serve hot.

Grilled Steak

Ingredients:

- 1 cup all-purpose flour
- ¾ cup cornmeal
- 1/3 cup sugar
- 2 teaspoons salt
- 1 teaspoon baking soda
- ½ cup onions, chopped
- 2 teaspoon jalapenos, chopped
- 1 cup buttermilk
- 2 large eggs
- ¼ cup unsalted butter
- 3 large tomatoes, chopped
- 1 small avocado, chopped
- 1 red onion, chopped
- 1 red bell pepper, chopped
- 1 lemon, juiced
- 1 tablespoon olive oil
- Salt to taste
- Pepper to taste

Instructions:

1. Open the grill, start the smoker and allow a fire to establish.
2. Set the temperature to 350 F and close the lid for 10 minutes.
3. Add the flour, cornmeal, sugar, salt, baking powder and baking soda to a bowl and mix until well combined.
4. Add in the onions and jalapenos and mix well.
5. Add to a greased 13x9x2 pan and add to the grill for 25 minutes or until a skewer inserted in the center comes out clean.
6. Tear the cornbread into small pieces.
7. Add the steak to a bowl and toss with salt and pepper.
8. Add it to the grill and grill for 30 minutes or until the internal temperature reaches 120 F.
9. Remove for 10 minutes and close the grill.
10. Add the steaks back and grill until the internal temperature reaches 130 F.

11. In the meantime add the tomatoes, avocado, onion, and pepper along with the cornbread and mix well.
12. Drizzle the olive oil and lemon juice all over it and mix well.
13. Add the steaks to a plate and top off with this mixture and serve hot.

Coffee Ribeye Steak

Ingredients:

- 1 pound rib eye steak
- ⅓ cup chili powder
- ¼ cup ground espresso
- 2 tablespoons paprika
- 2 tablespoons brown sugar
- 1 tablespoon dry mustard
- Salt to taste
- Pepper to taste
- 1 tablespoon coriander powder
- 1 tablespoon oregano powder

For salad

- 2 whole corn cobs
- ¼ cup olive oil
- ¼ cup white vinegar
- 12 to 15 basil leaves
- 12 to 15 mint leaves
- 10 to 12 thyme leaves
- 2 garlic cloves, minced

Instructions:

1. Open the lid of the smoker grill and allow a fire to establish.
2. Set the temperature to 450 F and close the lid.
3. Add the chili powder, coffee powder, paprika, brown sugar, mustard, salt, pepper, coriander and oregano to a bowl and mix until well combined.
4. Add the steak to a plate and top it with the rub and mix well.
5. Place the steak on the grill for 10 minutes or until the internal temperature reaches 135 F.
6. Meanwhile, add the corn to the grill and grill it on all sides.
7. Add a griddle to the grill and add the basil leaves, mint leaves, thyme and ginger and roast until brown.
8. Add them to a blender along with the olive oil and whizz until smooth.
9. Add the steak to a plate with the corn on the side and pour the herb mix all over.

Grilled Tri Tip

Ingredients:

- 1 pound tri tip
- ½ cup olive oil
- 1 large onion, chopped
- 3 tablespoons garlic, minced
- ¼ cup balsamic vinegar
- 1 teaspoon cayenne pepper
- Salt to taste
- Pepper to taste

Instructions:

1. Add the olive oil, onion, garlic, vinegar, cayenne pepper, salt, and pepper to a bowl and mix well.
2. Add the tri tip to the bowl and allow it to marinate for 6 to 8 hours.
3. Open the lid of the grill and allow a fire to establish.
4. Set the temperature to 350 and close the lid for 10 to 15 minutes.
5. Add it to the grill until the internal temperature to reaches 130 F.
6. Slice and serve.

Buttery Ribeye

Ingredients:

- 2 rib eyes, bone in
- Salt to taste
- Pepper to taste
- 4 tablespoons butter

Instructions:

1. Add the steak to a plate and sprinkle the salt and pepper on top.
2. Open the lid of the grill and allow a fire to establish.
3. Set the temperature to 450 F and close lid for 10 minutes.
4. Add the steak and grill for 15 minutes.
5. Add a griddle to the grill and add in the butter.
6. Once the butter melts, add the steak in with the grill side facing up.
7. Allow it to cook for 5 to 7 minutes.
8. Close the lid to cook the steak until the internal temperature reaches 130 F.
9. Remove out and allow it to rest for 10 minutes.
10. Slice and serve.

Smoked Beef Burger

Ingredients:

For burger

- 2 pounds beef mince
- 1 teaspoon rib rub
- 4 to 5 slices cheese
- 4 to 5 burger buns

For chili

- 1 pound beef mince
- 2 tablespoons chili powder
- 1 teaspoon paprika
- 1 teaspoon cumin
- 1 teaspoon oregano
- 1 teaspoon brown sugar
- 1 onion, chopped
- 2 teaspoon garlic, minced
- Salt to taste
- Pepper to taste
- 1 tablespoon cayenne pepper
- 1 cup beef stock
- 1 cup tomatoes, chopped

For salad

- ½ cabbage, shredded
- ½ cup purple cabbage, shredded
- 2 carrots, shredded
- ½ cup mayonnaise
- ½ cup cream
- 2 tablespoons vinegar
- Salt to taste
- Pepper to taste

Instructions:

1. Open the lid of the smoker grill and allow a fire to establish.
2. Add a griddle to the grill and add the beef mince.
3. Add the chili powder, paprika, cumin, oregano, brown sugar, garlic, salt, pepper, cayenne, beef stock and tomatoes and mix until well combined.
4. Reduce the heat down and cook for 20 minutes.
5. To make the patties, divide the meat into 4 balls and flatten between palms.
6. Add it to the grill for 5 minutes on each side.
7. The internal temperature should reach 140 F.
8. Add the cheese on top a few minutes before removing the patties from the grill.
9. Meanwhile, add the mayonnaise, sour cream, salt, pepper, and vinegar to a bowl and mix well.
10. Apply it inside the buns.
11. To assemble the burger, place the buns on the burger patty and top with additional cheese prepared chili and serve.

Beef Brisket

Ingredients:

- 6 pounds beef brisket
- 5 tablespoons rosemary
- 2 tablespoons cumin powder
- 2 tablespoons coriander powder
- 1 tablespoon oregano
- 2 teaspoons cinnamon powder
- Salt to taste
- 1 cup beef stock

Instructions:

1. Add the rosemary, cumin powder, coriander powder, oregano and cinnamon powder, salt to a bowl and mix until well combined.
2. Add the brisket to it and place in the fridge for 12 hours.
3. Open the lid of the smoker grill and allow a fire to establish.
4. Set the temperature to 250 F and close the lid for 15 minutes.
5. Add the beef to the grill and cook for 4 hours.
6. The internal temperature should reach 160 F.
7. Once done, add it to a foil and add the beef stock.
8. Add the foil back to the grill until the internal temperature reaches 200 F.
9. Remove from grill and allow it to cool for 30 minutes before serving.

Beef Jerky

Ingredients:

- 3 cups soya sauce
- 2 cups brown sugar
- 3 garlic cloves, chopped
- 1-inch ginger minced
- 1 tablespoon sesame oil
- 4-pound skirt steak

Instructions:

1. Add the soya sauce, brown sugar, garlic, ginger and sesame oil to a blender and whizz until smooth.
2. Clean the steak and slice it thinly along the grain.
3. Add to a bag along with the marinade and shake until well combined.
4. Open the lid of the smoker grill and allow a fire to establish.
5. Set the temperature to 450 and close lid for 10 minutes.
6. Add the steak to the grill until the internal temperature reaches 160 F.
7. Cook for 5 hours.

Beef Tacos

Ingredients:

- 4 pounds beef brisket
- ½ cup beef broth
- 15 tortillas
- 6 avocados
- 5 tomatoes, chopped
- 1 jalapeno, chopped
- 1 small onion, chopped
- ½ cup cream
- 1 lemon, juiced
- Salt to taste
- Pepper to taste

Instructions:

1. Open the grill, start the smoker and allow a fire to establish.
2. Set the temperature to 300 F and close lid for 15 minutes.
3. Slice the brisket against the grain.
4. And add to foil with the broth.
5. Close it tightly.
6. Add to a grill for 60 minutes.
7. Meanwhile, add the avocados, tomatoes, jalapenos, onion, cream, lemon juice, salt and pepper to a bowl and mix until well combined.
8. Place the tortillas on aluminum foil and fold it over.
9. Place this over the grill for 15 minutes.
10. Once done, add the beef in the center followed by the guacamole and serve.

Long Island Patties

Ingredients:

- 1 pound beef mince
- 2 tablespoons butter
- 2 onions, chopped
- 1 tablespoon yellow mustard
- 8 to 10 slices bread
- 8 to 10 slices cheese
- Salt to taste
- Pepper to taste
- Pickles

Instructions:

1. Open the lid of the grill and allow a fire to establish.
2. Set the temperature to 375 F and close the lid for 10 minutes.
3. Cut the onion into thin slices and add to a pan along with the butter.
4. Do not stir it and sprinkle salt and pepper on top to caramelize the onions.
5. Meanwhile, make patties using the beef mince and add to the grill to grill on both sides.
6. Add the patties to a grill until the internal temperature reaches 165 F.
7. Remove and place a griddle on the grill.
8. Add some butter and add the bread along with the cheese, patty, and onions followed by another slice of cheese.
9. Apply a thin layer of mustard on top, and the do the same with the other buns.
10. Flip the burgers once before adding to a plate.
11. Serve hot.

Horseradish Ribeye

Ingredients:

- 5 lb. Ribeye
- 5 garlic cloves, chopped
- ½ cup horseradish
- Salt to taste
- Pepper to taste
- ½ cup olive oil
- ½ bunch rosemary leaves
- ½ bunch thyme leaves

Instructions:

1. Open the lid of the smoker grill and allow a fire to establish.
2. Set the temperature to 350 and close the lid for 15 minutes.
3. Add the garlic, horseradish, salt, pepper, olive oil, rosemary and thyme leaves to a blender and whizz until smooth.
4. Add it to a plate along with the ribs and massage it in.
5. Add it to the grill and roast for 2 hours.
6. The internal temperature should reach about 165 F.
7. Remove the beef out and allow it to sit for 20 minutes.
8. Serve hot.

Beefy Meatballs

Ingredients:

- 4 slices whole wheat bread
- ½ cup milk
- 24 ounces beef mince
- 1 large onion, chopped
- 1 large egg, beaten
- 1 teaspoon all spice powder
- Salt to taste
- Pepper to taste

For relish

- 2 tablespoons butter
- 2 tablespoons olive oil
- 1 tablespoon flour
- 1 cup sodium broth
- ¼ cup cream
- 1 cup cranberries
- 2 teaspoons sugar
- 1 teaspoon lemon zest
- 1 tablespoon ginger
- 2 tablespoons parsley leaves
- 2 tablespoon dill leaves

Instructions:

1. Add the butter to a mixer and mix until soft.
2. Add in the beef, onion and egg and mix until well combined.
3. Add the allspice, salt, and pepper and mix well.
4. Dip your palm in cold water and pick up small portions of the beef mix to make small balls.
5. Open the lid of the grill and allow a fire to establish.
6. Set the temperature to 375 F and close the lid for 10 minutes.

7. Place a skillet on the grill and add in a tablespoon of butter along with a tablespoon of oil.
8. Add half of the meatballs and cook for 2 minutes.
9. Flip them over to brown on the other side for 2 minutes.
10. Remove them and repeat with the remaining balls.
11. Add in the rest of the butter and oil along with the flour and mix until combined.
12. Add the chicken broth and cream and whisk until combined.
13. Add the meatballs back to the gravy and mix gently.
14. Toss in the salt and pepper and mix slowly.
15. To make the relish, add the cranberries, sugar, lemon zest, lemon juice and ginger to a blender and mix until well combined.
16. Add in salt and sugar to it and remove to a bowl.
17. Add the meatballs to a platter and pour the mix on top.

Smoked Lamb

Ingredients:

- 1 lamb leg, trimmed
- Salt to taste
- Pepper to taste
- 1 garlic head, chopped
- 2 tablespoons rosemary, chopped
- ¼ bottle dry wine

For salsa verde

- 5 garlic cloves, minced
- 1 tablespoon capers
- 1 pound tomatoes, chopped
- 1 onion, chopped
- 5 chilies
- ¼ cup cilantro leaves, chopped
- 1 teaspoon sugar
- Salt to taste
- 2 tablespoons olive oil
- 1 cup chicken broth
- 3 tablespoons lemon juice

Instructions:

1. Open the lid of the grill and allow a fire to establish.
2. Set the temperature to 350 F and close the lid for 10 minutes.
3. Add the garlic, tomato, onion, and chilies to a skewer and place on grill for 10 minutes or until brown spots form.
4. Allow to cool down for some time before removing the skins from the vegetables.
5. Add it to a blender along with the tomatoes, cilantro, and sugar and make a fine paste.
6. Add oil to a pan and add in the tomato paste.
7. Add the broth and lime juice and wait for it to thicken.
8. Simmer for some time and switch off.
9. Make small cuts over the lamb using a sharp knife and place a garlic clove each.

10. Sprinkle with salt, pepper, and rosemary and rub over the lamb.
11. Add the lamb to the grill and close for 30 minutes.
12. The internal temperature should reach 130 F.
13. Add it to a cutting board and allow it to rest for some time before cutting.

Smoked Sausages

Ingredients:

- 2 pounds lamb shoulder
- 1 teaspoon paprika
- 1 tablespoon parsley, chopped
- 60 inches hog casing
- ½ teaspoon cayenne pepper
- Salt to taste
- Pepper to taste
- 1 tablespoon cilantro, chopped

For sauce

- 3 cups yogurt
- 1 garlic, minced
- 1 cucumber, shredded
- 1 tablespoon dill leaves
- Salt to taste
- Pepper to taste

Instructions:

1. Cut the lamb into 2-inch pieces and add to a grinder to make a mince.
2. Add the mince to a bowl along with spices and mix well.
3. Using a sausage horn, attach the casing to one end and start feeding the mince in through the other.
4. Twist the casing every few minutes and use a knife to make holes here and there.
5. Open the grill, start the smoker and wait for a fire to establish.
6. Set the temperature to 275 F.
7. Place the sausages on the grill for 5 to 10 minutes or until crisp.
8. Serve hot.

Smoked Lamb Shank

Ingredients:

- 4 lamb shanks
- 1 bottle rib tub
- 1 cup red wine
- Olive oil to drizzle
- 1 cup beef broth
- 5 sprigs rosemary and thyme

Instructions:

1. Make 4 equal sized squares from the aluminum foil and place on a table.
2. Place the shanks on the foil and add oil on top.
3. Sprinkle the rub on top.
4. Close the foil on three sides and leave one side open.
5. Open the lid and allow a fire to establish.
6. Place the lamb on the grill and smoke for an hour.
7. Pour the wine inside the packet along with the rosemary and thyme and cover.
8. Place it back on the grill.
9. The internal temperature should reach 180 F.
10. Open the pack and serve hot.

Lamb Lollipops

Ingredients:

- 5 lamb chops
- 2 tablespoons olive oil
- Salt to taste
- Pepper to taste
- 2 tablespoons mint, chopped

For chutney

- 1 large mango, chopped
- 3 sprigs cilantro
- Salt to taste
- Pepper to taste
- 3 garlic cloves, chopped
- Lime juice
- ½ habanero chile, chopped

Instructions:

1. Buy fresh lamb chops. If you can't find them, then use a sharp knife to push back the fat and flesh from the chops.
2. Add the mango, cilantro, salt, pepper, garlic, lime juice and habanero to a blender and whizz until smooth.
3. Open the grill, start the smoker and allow a fire to establish.
4. Set the temperature to 375 F and close the lid for 10 minutes.
5. Add the lamb to a foil and sprinkle with salt and pepper.
6. Add the lamb to the grill and grill it for 3 minutes on each side or until the temperature reaches 130 F.
7. Remove and allow it to rest for 10 minutes before adding the mango chutney on top.
8. Cut and serve.

Pistachio with Lamb

Ingredients:

- 2 lamb racks
- 1 tablespoon oil
- 1 tablespoon butter
- Salt to taste
- Pepper to taste
- 3 tablespoons mustard
- 2 tablespoons breadcrumbs

For carrots and potatoes

- 1 pound potatoes
- Salt to taste
- 2 garlic cloves, chopped
- 1 big bunch carrots
- 2 teaspoons thyme
- 1 tablespoon olive oil

Instructions:

1. Open the lid of the grill and allow a fire to establish.
2. Set the temperature to high and close lid for 10 minutes.
3. Pat the lamb dry and sprinkle with salt and pepper.
4. Peel the carrots and add to a bowl along with the potatoes.
5. Add the pepper, oil, and salt and mix well.
6. Add a skillet to the grill and add in oil.
7. Add in the vegetables and sauté for some time.
8. Add the lamb to the skillet and brown on all sides.
9. Add the pistachios, salt, and pepper to a bowl.
10. Apply the mustard to the lamb and sprinkle the pistachios on top.
11. Place the lamb on the grill and brown.
12. Cover the lamb with foil.
13. Give the potatoes and carrots a stir.
14. Close and cook for 10 minutes or until internal temperature reaches 125 F.
15. Remove and allow to cool for 10 minutes.
16. Slice and serve.

Greek Lamb

Ingredients:

- 7-pound leg of lamb
- 8 to 10 garlic cloves
- 1 bunch rosemary leaves
- 5 tablespoons olive oil
- 2 lemons, juiced
- Salt to taste
- Pepper to taste

Instructions:

1. Use a sharp knife to make several small incisions in the leg of the lamb.
2. Add the garlic, rosemary, and oregano to a blender and whizz to a smooth paste.
3. Add the paste inside the slits of the lamb.
4. Drizzle the lemon juice and olive oil over the lamb and rub evenly.
5. Cover and place in the fridge for 10 hours or overnight.
6. Remove and sprinkle with salt and pepper.
7. Open the grill, start the smoker and allow a fire to establish.
8. Raise the temperature to 400 F and roast for 10 minutes.
9. Reduce the temperature to 350 F and cook for 30 minutes.
10. The internal temperature should reach 140 F.
11. Add to a plate and wait to cool down before cutting and serving.

Lamb Stew

Ingredients:

- 3 tablespoons olive oil
- 2 cups beef stock
- 3 carrots, chopped
- 2 pounds lamb chunks, chopped
- 2 garlic cloves, chopped
- Salt to taste
- Pepper to taste
- ¼ cup tomato puree
- 5 tablespoons thyme leaves
- 5 tablespoon rosemary leaves
- 10 ounces beer
- 1 large turnip, chopped
- 1 large parsnip, chopped

Instructions:

1. Open the lid of the grill and allow a fire to establish.
2. Set the temperature at 450 F and close lid for 10 minutes.
3. Add the lamb to a plate and season with salt and pepper.
4. Add a Dutch oven to the grill and add in 1-tablespoon oil.
5. Add the lamb to the oven and brown on both sides.
6. Add the garlic and sauté for 2 minutes.
7. Add in the tomato puree and mix well.
8. Add the beef stock, beer, thyme leaves, rosemary leaves, salt and pepper and mix well.
9. Add in the turnip and parsnips and cover to cook for an hour.
10. Serve hot.

Armenian Lamb

Ingredients:

- 2 tablespoons honey
- ¼ cup tomato puree
- 2 garlic cloves, chopped
- 1 teaspoon fenugreek powder
- 1 teaspoon cumin powder
- 1 tablespoon cayenne powder
- 1 teaspoon cinnamon powder
- 1 teaspoon turmeric powder
- Salt to taste
- 4 lamb shanks
- 2 quarts lamb stock
- 1 cup barley
- 2 tablespoons olive oil
- 1 onion, chopped
- ½ cup parmesan cheese
- 2 tablespoons butter

Instructions:

1. Add the honey, tomato paste, garlic, cinnamon, fenugreek, cumin, cayenne, turmeric, and salt to bowl and mix until well combined.
2. Prepare the lamb by removing the skin and toning down the tendons.
3. Open the grill, start the smoker and allow a fire to establish.
4. Set the temperature to 300 F and close for 10 minutes.
5. Place a skillet on the grill and add the lamb shanks.
6. Cook for 8 hours and keep turning the shanks every few minutes.
7. With an hour to go for the lamb, start making the risotto.
8. Add the stock to a griddle and add the barley.
9. Bring it to a boil and set aside.
10. Add the oil to a pan and toss in the onions to sauté.
11. Add in the barley with the stock and mix.
12. The barley should fully absorb the stock.
13. Add in the salt and mix well.
14. Add in the cheese and butter and mix well.
15. Add the lamb to a plate along with the risotto and serve hot.

Slow Roast Shoulder

Ingredients:

- 1 teaspoon coriander seeds
- 1 teaspoon cumin seeds
- 1 teaspoon mint leaves
- 2 ounces anchovies
- 1 tablespoon smoked paprika
- 1 tablespoon lemon juice 2 garlic cloves, chopped
- ¼ cup olive oil
- Salt to taste
- 3 pounds lamb shoulder, bone in

Instructions:

1. Add the coriander and cumin seeds to a blender and make a fine powder.
2. Add the chilies and water to hot water and allow it to soak for 10 minutes.
3. Add the chilies to a blender along with the spices, paprika, garlic, oil and salt and whizz to a small paste.
4. Add the lamb to a pan and smear the harissa over it and place for 2 hours.
5. Open the lid of the grill and allow a fire to establish.
6. Set the temperature to 325 F and close lid for 10 minutes.
7. Add a griddle to the grill and add in lamb stock.
8. Add the lamb steak to it and pour the water over it.
9. Cook for 20 to 30 minutes.
10. Meanwhile, add the yogurt, cilantro leaves, garlic and oil to a bowl and mix well.
11. Add the lamb to a plate and add the yogurt on top.
12. Add the remaining harissa on top and serve.

Butter Grilled Lamb

Ingredients:

- ¼ cup wine
- Salt to taste
- 1 large onion, chopped
- Salt to taste
- Pepper to taste
- 1 cup olive oil
- 5-pound leg of lamb
- 2 tablespoons thyme leaves
- 1 large lemon, juiced

Instructions:

1. Add the vinegar, garlic, thyme, rosemary salt and pepper to a bowl and mix well.
2. Add in the oil and mix until well combined.
3. Add the lamb to a bag and pour in the marinade.
4. Add in the onions and rind and shake until combined.
5. Open the grill, start the smoker and wait for a fire to establish.
6. Set the temperature to 450 F and close the lid for 5 minutes.
7. Place the lamb on the grill with the fat on the bottom.
8. The internal temperature should reach 135 F.
9. Slice with the grain and serve.

Rosemary Lamb

Ingredients:

- 10 pounds lamb leg, bone in
- 1 tablespoon garlic, chopped
- 1 bunch rosemary leaves
- 2 tablespoons olive oil
- 2 large lemons, juiced
- Salt to taste
- Pepper to taste

Instructions:

1. Add the olive oil and garlic to a bowl and crush using a fork.
2. Using a sharp knife, make incisions in the lamb.
3. Insert the rosemary leaves into the slits and also rub them all over the lamb.
4. Squeeze the lemon over the lamb and spread the juice evenly over it.
5. Sprinkle some zest and follow up with the garlic and oil mix.
6. Open the lid of the grill and allow a fire to establish.
7. Set the temperature to 400 F and close lid for 10 minutes.
8. Place the lamb on the grill for 30 minutes.
9. The internal temperature should reach 145 F.
10. Allow the lamb to cool for 10 minutes before carving and serving.

Lamb Wraps

Ingredients:

- 7 pounds leg of lamb
- 1 lemon, juiced
- 2 tablespoons olive oil
- Salt to taste
- Pepper to taste
- 1 bottle game rub
- 12 pita bread
- Roma tomatoes, chopped
- 1 onion, chopped
- 10 ounces cheese

For Greek sauce

- 2 cups yogurt
- 2 zucchinis
- 2 garlic cloves, chopped
- 2 lemons, squeezed
- 4 tablespoons dill leaves
- 2 tablespoons mint leaves
- Salt to taste
- Pepper to taste

Instructions:

1. Add lemon juice and olive oil to a bowl and mix well.
2. Apply it over the lamb and rub well.
3. Open the lid and allow a fire to establish.
4. Set the temperature to 400 F and close the lid for 10 minutes.
5. Add the lamb and roast it for 30 minutes.
6. The internal temperature of the lamb should reach 140 F.
7. Meanwhile, add the yogurt to a bowl along with the lemon juice, garlic, dill leaves, mint leaves, salt and pepper and mix well.

8. Add in chopped zucchini and mix until well combined.
9. Place it in the fridge until serving.
10. Spread a few pitas over the foil and place it on the grill for 10 minutes.
11. Add the lamb to a cutting board and cut it into pieces.
12. Add the lamb to the pitas followed by the salad and cheese crumbled on top.

Apricot Lamb

Ingredients:

- 6 pounds lamb leg, bone in
- Grill seasoning
- 2 garlic cloves, chopped
- 10 ounces apricot spread
- ¼ cup horseradish

Instructions:

1. Add the lamb leg to a plate and sprinkle it generously with the seasoning.
2. Rub vigorously to spread it all over the meat.
3. Open the lid of the grill and allow a fire to establish.
4. Set the temperature to 400 F.
5. Place a griddle on the grill and add in the garlic, apricot spread, and horseradish.
6. Remove the griddle and add the lamb to the grill.
7. Use a brush to apply the glaze over the lamb.
8. Close the lid for 15 minutes before flipping it over and applying glaze on the other side.
9. The internal temperature of the lamb should reach 140 F.
10. Serve warm.

Lamb Lollipops in Honey Mustard Sauce

Ingredients:

- ½ cup olive oil
- ¼ cup onions, chopped
- 2 garlic cloves, chopped
- 2 tablespoons soy sauce
- 2 tablespoons balsamic vinegar
- 1 tablespoon rosemary leaves
- 1 cup honey
- ¼ cup mustard
- 1 teaspoon sauce
- Salt to taste
- Pepper to taste

Instructions:

1. Open grill lid and allow a fire to establish.
2. Set the temperature to 450 F and close the lid for 10 minutes.
3. Add a pan to the grill.
4. Add the oil, onions, and garlic to a pan and sauté for a few minutes.
5. Move the ingredients to a blender along with the honey and mustard and whizz until smooth.
6. Add the lamb to a plate and brush with oil on all sides.
7. Sprinkle the salt and pepper and rub.
8. Add it to a grill and turn every few minutes.
9. The internal temperature should reach 135 F.
10. Add the lamb to a plate and drizzle the honey mustard on top.
11. Serve hot.

Chapter 6: Pork Recipes Using a Wood Pellet-Smoker Grill

Barbeque Ribs

Ingredients:

- 1 rack pork ribs
- Salt to taste
- Pepper to taste
- ½ cup barbecue sauce
- 1 pound potatoes
- 2 tablespoons oil
- 5 eggs, boiled
- ½ cup sour cream
- 1 tablespoon dill leaves
- 1 tablespoon parsley leaves
- 2 onions, chopped
- 1/4 cup apple juice

Instructions:

1. Add the pork ribs to a plate and sprinkle the salt and pepper on top.
2. Open the lid and allow a fire to establish.
3. Set the temperature to 250 F and close the lid for 10 minutes.
4. Place the ribs on the grill and cook for 3 hours.
5. Once done, sprinkle apple juice over the ribs.
6. Close the lid for an hour.
7. Apply some barbecue sauce over the ribs and close for 2 hours.
8. Meanwhile, add the potatoes to a bowl along with the olive oil, salt, pepper, and add to the grill.
9. Add the potatoes to a bowl along with the eggs, cream, dill leaves, parsley, and onions and mix well.
10. Add the lamb rack to a plate and cut into individual ribs.
11. Add the salad on top and serve.

Smoked Bacon Sandwich

Ingredients:

- 2 pounds thick cut bacon
- 2 lettuce heads
- ½ cup mayonnaise
- 3 tomatoes, chopped
- 8 to 10 toast

Instructions:

1. Open the grill, start the smoker and allow a fire to establish.
2. Set the temperature to 350 F and close the lid for 10 minutes.
3. Once the grill heat, add the bacon to it and grill on both sides for 20 minutes or until crispy.
4. To make the sandwich, add the mayonnaise inside the bread and spread evenly.
5. Add the lettuce leaves on top followed by the tomatoes, bacon and place another slice of bread on top.
6. Serve warm.

WOOD PELLET SMOKER AND GRILL COOKBOOK

Smoked Pork Sausage Dogs

Ingredients:

- 1 large onion, chopped
- 2 jalapenos, chopped
- Salt to taste
- Pepper to taste
- 4 pork sausages
- 4 hot dogs
- 8 ounces cream cheese
- 1 tablespoon mustard

Instructions:

1. Open the grill, start the smoker and allow a fire to establish.
2. Set the temperature to 450 F and close the lid for 10 minutes.
3. Add the jalapenos, Frank sausages and onions to the grill and grill on both sides.
4. Add them to a chopping board and chop them finely before adding salt and mixing.
5. Add cream cheese inside the buns and place a hot dog in the center.
6. Add the cream cheese on top of each and top off with the jalapenos and onions.
7. Serve warm.

Barbecue Pork Shoulder

Ingredients:

- 8-pound pork butt, bone in
- 4 tablespoons sugar
- 1 tablespoon salt
- 2 cups apple juice
- ¼ cup pork rub
- Barbecue sauce as needed

Instructions:

1. Add the pork to a cutting board and trim away excess fat.
2. Add the pork rub, apple juice, sugar and salt to a bowl and mix until well combined.
3. Make small slits in the pork and add to the juice mixture.
4. Pour the remainder over the pork and rub well.
5. Open the lid of the grill and allow a fire to establish.
6. Set the temperature to 250 F and close the lid for 10 minutes.
7. Add the pork butt to the grill and roast for 6 hours.
8. The internal temperature should reach 165 F.
9. Once done, add the pork to a tin foil and pour the apple juice over it.
10. Tightly wrap the foil and place on a grill.
11. Increase the temperature to 275 F.
12. Cook for 3 hours or until the temperature reaches 195 F.
13. Remove from grill and allow it to rest for 10 minutes.
14. Slice and serve hot.

Pork with Peaches

Ingredients:

- 2 tablespoon olive oil
- 4 peaches, pitted and chopped
- 2 onions, chopped
- 2 cups whiskey
- 1 cup orange juice
- ¾ cup vinegar
- ½ cup white wine
- ½ cup honey
- Salt to taste
- Pepper to taste
- 4 double cut pork chops
- 3 tablespoons pork rub

Instructions:

1. Open the grill, start the smoker and allow a fire to establish.
2. Set the temperature to 375 F and close the lid for 10 minutes.
3. Add a pan to the grill.
4. To make the whiskey sauce, add the whiskey, orange juice, white wine, honey, salt, and pepper to the pan and bring to a boil.
5. For the peaches, add a cast iron pan to the grill and add in oil.
6. Add the peaches, onions, and scallions over it.
7. Wait for them to caramelize and the scallions to soften for about 15 minutes.
8. To make the pork, sprinkle with rub and add to a grill.
9. Close the lid for 30 minutes.
10. The internal temperature should reach 140 F.
11. Serve the chops on a plate along with the peaches, scallions, and onions and pour the whiskey sauce on top.

Molasses Glazed Pork

Ingredients:

- 5 pounds pork shoulder
- Salt to taste
- Pepper to taste
- 2 cups molasses
- 2 tablespoons mustard

For sauce

- ¼ cup olive oil
- 1 cup tomatoes, crushed
- 8 ounces bell peppers
- 1 tablespoon smoked paprika
- 3 tablespoons vinegar
- 2 tablespoons mint leaves
- 5 garlic cloves, chopped
- Salt to taste
- Pepper to taste
- ½ cup almonds
- 1 thick, crusty bread

Instructions:

- Open the grill, start the smoker and allow a fire to establish.
- Set the temperature to 225 F and close the lid for 10 minutes.
- Add the pork to a plate and sprinkle with salt and pepper.
- Add it to the grill and roast for 6 hours.
- To make the sauce, add the almonds, bread, garlic, and oil to a pan and toast until golden.
- Add it to a food processor and grind to a paste.
- Toss in the salt, pepper and pour in the vinegar.
- Add the mint leaves and remove to a bowl.
- Add the molasses and mustard to a bowl and set aside.
- With an hour to go, open the lid of the grill and apply the mustard on top.
- The roast should reach an internal temperature of 180 F.
- Remove to a cutting board and allow it to cool for 10 minutes.
- Slice and serve.

Pork Shoulder Nachos

Ingredients:

- 9 pounds pork butt, bone in
- 2 cups cider vinegar
- 1 bottle game rub

For cheese sauce

- 5 tablespoons butter
- 4 cups milk
- ¼ cup flour
- 2 cups cheddar cheese
- 2 cups parmesan cheese

Instructions:

1. Open the lid and allow a fire to establish.
2. Set the temperature to 250 F and close the lid for 10 minutes.
3. Cut off any excess fat from the pork butt and sprinkle with salt and pepper.
4. Add the pork to the grill and cook until the internal temperature reaches 160 F.
5. Meanwhile, make the cheese sauce by adding butter to a pan along with flour to create a thick mixture.
6. Add in the milk and simmer until thick.
7. Add the cheddar and Parmesan cheese and mix until well combined.
8. Add the pork to an aluminum foil and wrap it with one side open.
9. Pour in the vinegar and add back to the grill.
10. Cook for 3 hours or until the internal temperature reaches 200 F.
11. Remove the pork and allow it to cool down for an hour.
12. Add it to a grill and use a fork to pull it apart.
13. Add the nachos to a plate and sprinkle the pork on top.
14. Drizzle the cheese mixture over it.

Pork Stuffed Apples

Ingredients:

- 10 large apples
- 5 tablespoon butter
- 1 large onion, chopped
- 1 celery rib, chopped
- 12 ounces chorizo
- 4 tablespoons orange glaze
- Salt to taste
- Pepper to taste

Instructions:

1. Open the lid of the grill smoker and allow a fire to establish.
2. Set the temperature to 275 and close the lid for 10 minutes.
3. Add a skillet over the grill.
4. Add the butter to a skillet and allow it to melt.
5. Add in the onions and celery and cook them until golden.
6. Add in the chorizo and brown for 10 minutes.
7. Remove the fat from the pan and toss in salt and pepper.
8. Meanwhile, use a spoon to remove cores from the apple.
9. Add about a spoonful of the mixture inside each apple place a knob of butter over it.
10. Place the apples on the grate for an hour.
11. Once done, allow it to cool for 5 minutes before serving warm.

Pork Mac and Cheese

Ingredients:

- 3 pounds pork belly, skin removed and scored
- Salt to taste
- 4 tablespoons sugar
- Pepper to taste

For mac and cheese

- 1 tablespoon olive oil
- 4 tablespoons butter
- 4 tablespoons flour
- 2 cups milk
- 3 cups cheddar cheese
- 1 teaspoon nutmeg
- 1 teaspoon cayenne pepper
- 1 pound macaroni
- 1 onion, chopped
- 1 tablespoon garlic, chopped

Instructions:

1. For the pork, add the salt, pepper to a bowl and sprinkle over the pork.
2. Place in fridge for 12 hours or overnight.
3. Open the grill, start the smoker and allow a fire to establish.
4. Set the temperature to 250 F and close the lid for an hour.
5. Allow the pork to reach room temperature before adding to the grill.
6. Cook for 2 hours or until the pork has tenderized.
7. Allow it to cool down before adding to a foil and wrapping tightly.
8. For the mac and cheese, add water and salt to a pot and bring to a boil.
9. Add in the noodles and cook until they tenderize.
10. Add a pan to the grill pour in the olive oil.
11. Add the butter, onions and sauté until they tenderize.
12. Once done, sprinkle the flour and stir until combined.

13. Once done, add in the garlic, and flour and mix until a roux forms.
14. Stir in the milk and keep whisking.
15. Add in the nutmeg and cayenne and mix until well combined.
16. Add in the noodles and mix well.
17. Chop the pork into small pieces and add it to the noodles.
18. Serve warm.

Smoked Sausage Rolls

Ingredients:

- 2 pounds bacon
- 2 pounds breakfast sausage
- 10 ounces cream cheese
- 4 jalapenos, chopped
- 2 tablespoons jalapeno jelly
- ¼ cup game rub
- ½ cup spicy sauce

Instructions:

1. Open the lid of the grill and allow a fire to establish.
2. Set the temperature to 275 F and close the lid for 10 minutes.
3. Add the waxed paper to a board and add the breakfast sausages to it.
4. Flatten it out using a rolling pin.
5. Add the cream cheese, jalapenos, and jalapeno jelly to a bowl and mix until well combined.
6. Spread the mixture over the sausages.
7. Roll the sausages into a roll so that the filling stays put.
8. Wrap the bacon around the sausage roll.
9. Sprinkle the rub on top of it.
10. Place the roll on the grill for about an hour.
11. Serve warm.

WOOD PELLET SMOKER AND GRILL COOKBOOK

Pork with Pineapple

Ingredients:

- 1 large pineapple
- 2 tablespoons rub
- 1 pound thick cut bacon
- 2 pork ribs
- ¼ cup Cajun dressing

Instructions:

1. Cut the top and bottom of the pineapple and cut away the skin.
2. Cut the pineapple vertically and remove the core from the center.
3. Add to a bowl and sprinkle the rub on top.
4. Join the two pineapple halves together.
5. Place strips of bacon over the pineapple and wrap them around.
6. Insert a toothpick into the bacon to secure it to the pineapple.
7. Continue on all sides until the pineapple is completely wrapped in bacon.
8. Open the lid of the grill and allow a fire to establish.
9. Set the temperature to 275 F and close the lid for 10 minutes.
10. Add the pineapple over the grate and wait for the temperature to reach 160 F.
11. Allow it to cool for 5 minutes before slicing and serving.

Pork Multigrain Sandwiches

Ingredients:

- 1 cup olives
- 1 tablespoon oregano
- Salt to taste
- Pepper to taste
- ½ cup bell peppers
- 3 tablespoons wine
- 5 garlic cloves, chopped
- 3 tablespoons capers

For sandwich

- 10 slices multigrain bread
- ⅓ pound prosciutto ham
- ⅓ pound salami
- ¼ pound mozzarella cheese
- ⅓ pound provolone cheese

Instructions:

1. Open the lid of the grill and allow a fire to establish.
2. Set the temperature to 250 F.
3. Place a cheese slice on the grill.
4. Add the olives, oregano, salt, pepper, bell pepper, wine, garlic, and capers to a bowl and mix until well combined
5. Add a pan to the grill and place the bread slices to lightly toast them.
6. To make the sandwich, arrange the bread on a plate and add a tablespoon of the olive salad on top.
7. Place a ham, salami, and grilled cheese over it and cover with another slice of bread.
8. Serve warm.

Smoked Pork Ribs

Ingredients:

- 2 racks of pork ribs, bone in
- 5 ounces of game rub
- 8 ounces pineapple juice
- 1 bottle barbecue sauce

Instructions:

1. Add the pork to a plate and remove the membrane from the ribs.
2. Sprinkle the rub over the pork and rub gently.
3. Open the lid of the grill and allow a fire to establish.
4. Set the temperature to 225 F and close the lid for 120 minutes.
5. Place the ribs on the grill and gently pour the pineapple juice over it.
6. Close the lid and smoke the pork for an hour.
7. Cook for 4 hours or until the internal temperature reaches 200 F.
8. Once done, apply the barbecue sauce and let the pork sit for 10 minutes.
9. Slice the ribs and serve warm.

Pork Stew

Ingredients:

- 1 cup salsa verde
- 1 cup black beans
- 1 cup tomatoes, chopped
- 1 cup smoked pork, shredded
- 1 teaspoon cumin powder
- 2 cups sodium broth
- Salt to taste
- Pepper to taste

Instructions:

1. Open the lid of the grill and allow a fire to establish.
2. Set the temperature to 450 F and close the lid for 10 minutes.
3. Add a Dutch oven to the grill and add the salsa, tomatoes, pork, cumin, chicken broth, salt and pepper and mix until well combined.
4. Cover the oven and cook for an hour.
5. Serve with fresh avocado herbs and sour cream on top.

Eggs Benedict with Pork

Ingredients:

- 1 cup unsalted butter
- 3 egg yolks
- 1 tablespoon water
- 1 tablespoon lemon juice
- Salt to taste
- Pepper to taste
- 1 tablespoon chipotle sauce

For eggs Benedict

- Leftover pulled pork
- 6 poached eggs
- 1 tablespoon lemon juice
- 4 English muffins

Instructions:

1. Divide the butter into half and keep one-half in the fridge.
2. Add the butter to a pan and warm.
3. Beat the yolks until thick.
4. Add in the water, lemon juice, and butter and mix until well combined.
5. Add this to the melted butter and whisk until well combined.
6. Sprinkle the salt and pepper along with the chipotle sauce and mix until well combined.
7. Place the bowl in a pan containing hot water to poach the eggs.
8. Open the grill, start the smoker and allow a fire to establish.
9. Set the temperature to 325 F and place a pot.
10. Add water to the pot along with vinegar, lemon juice and crack in the eggs.
11. Once the water starts to boil stir the eggs around and take them out on a plate.
12. Brush the English muffins with butter and place on the grill for 3 minutes.
13. To assemble the dish, layer the muffin with pulled pork poached egg and the chipotle sauce and serve warm.

Pork with Strawberry Sauce

Ingredients:

- 2 pounds pork tenderloin
- 2 tablespoons rosemary leaves
- 2 tablespoons olive oil
- 1 cup balsamic vinegar
- 4 teaspoons sugar
- 10 strawberries, chopped
- Salt to taste
- Pepper to taste

Instructions:

1. Open the grill, start the smoker and allow a fire to establish.
2. Set the temperature to 350 F and close the lid for 10 minutes.
3. Clean and pat the pork dry.
4. Sprinkle with the salt and pepper and rub well.
5. Add a Dutch oven to the grill and heat the oil.
6. Add the pork to it and brown on all sides.
7. Add it to the grill and cook for 20 minutes or until the internal temperature reaches 160 F.
8. Remove from the grill and rest for 10 minutes.
9. Add the strawberries to the skillet and soften for a couple of minutes.
10. Add the vinegar and scrape out the brown bits stuck to the bottom.
11. Simmer it until the sauce thickens.
12. Slice the pork and add the strawberries on top.
13. Drizzle with the balsamic vinegar and serve hot.

Pork with Apple Glaze

Ingredients:

- ½ cup apple jelly
- 2 tablespoons butter
- 1 tablespoon mustard
- 2 teaspoon vinegar
- 1 teaspoon Worcestershire sauce
- 1 teaspoon cinnamon powder
- 4 pounds pork tenderloin
- Salt to taste
- Pepper to taste

Instructions:

1. To make the glaze, add the apple jelly to a saucepan and toss in the butter until it melts.
2. Add in the mustard, vinegar, Worcestershire sauce and cinnamon and mix until well combined.
3. Add in the salt and pepper and mix well.
4. Open the grill, start the smoker and allow a fire to establish.
5. Preheat it to 375 F for 10 minutes.
6. Add the pork to the grill and turn it around every 20 minutes.
7. Use a basting brush to baste the pork every 10 minutes.
8. Cook the pork until it reaches an internal temperature of 160 F.
9. Add the pork to a cutting board and wait for it to cool down before slicing and serving.

Pork Breakfast Bake

Ingredients:

- 2 pounds hash browns
- 1 pound breakfast sausage
- 1 pound bacon
- 2 green bell peppers
- 1 red bell pepper
- 2 cups cheddar cheese, shredded
- 8 whole eggs
- 1 cup whole milk
- Salt to taste
- Pepper to taste

Instructions:

1. Open the grill, start the smoker and allow a fire to establish.
2. Set the temperature to 350 F and close the lid for 10 minutes.
3. Add the bacon to the grill and crisp for 30 minutes.
4. Once done, remove and cut into bite sized pieces.
5. Cut the peppers into small pieces and grill for 15 minutes.
6. Add the hash browns, sausages, cooked bacon, bell peppers, cheese, salt, and pepper to a bowl and mix until well combined.
7. In another bowl, add the eggs, milk and pour it over the hash browns.
8. Cover it with foil and cook for 2 hours.
9. The internal temperature should reach 165 F.
10. Serve hot.

BBQ Ribs with Potato Salad

Ingredients:

- 1 rack ribs, trimmed and membrane removed
- Salt to taste
- Pepper to taste
- 1 pound potatoes
- 1 tablespoon parsley
- 1 tablespoon dill leaves
- 3 tablespoons vinegar
- ½ cup barbecue sauce

Instructions:

1. Add the pork to a plate and sprinkle with the rub.
2. Open the grill, start the smoker and allow a fire to establish.
3. Set the temperature to 250 F and close the lid for 10 minutes.
4. Place the ribs on the grill grate and cook covered for 3 hours.
5. After about an hour, apply the barbecue sauce and cover again to cook for 30 minutes.
6. Meanwhile, add the potatoes to a bowl and add the oil, salt, pepper, and place on a cookie sheet.
7. Place the sheet on the grill and grill for 30 minutes.
8. Remove it from the grill and add to a bowl.
9. Drizzle it with vinegar and add the sour cream, dill, and parsley and mix together.
10. Slice the ribs and serve with a heap of potato salad.

Prosciutto Wrapped Tenderloins

Ingredients:

- 2 pounds pork tenderloins
- ½ pound prosciutto ham, chopped
- ½ pound bacon

For rub

- 2 tablespoons olive oil
- 2 tablespoons rosemary, chopped
- 1 tablespoon garlic, chopped
- Salt to taste
- Pepper to taste

Instructions:

1. Trim off the excess skin and fat from the pork and set it aside.
2. Add the olive oil, rosemary, garlic, salt, and pepper to a bowl and mix until well combined.
3. Add it to the tenderloins and rub until well coated.
4. Spread a twine over the work surface and layer the bacon and pancetta over the twine.
5. Lay a slice of prosciutto ham over the bacon and pancetta and place the tenderloin on top of it.
6. Keep repeating this until you exhaust all the ingredients.
7. Tie the twine on top and make sure you make it a tight knot.
8. Open the grill, start the smoker and allow a fire to establish.
9. Set the temperature to 450 F and close for 10 minutes.
10. Place the prosciutto on the grill and cook for 20 minutes or until the internal temperature reaches 145 F.
11. Remove it from the grill and allow to cool for 5 minutes before slicing and serving.

Pork with Herbs

Ingredients:

- 2 pounds pork tenderloin
- 5 garlic cloves, chopped
- 1 lemon, juiced
- 2 sprigs rosemary
- 2 sprigs thyme
- 2 tablespoons soya sauce
- Salt to taste
- Pepper to taste
- Red pepper flakes
- ¼ cup olive oil

Instructions:

1. Use a sharp knife to trim the ends of the tenderloin and remove some of the fat.
2. Add the garlic, lemon juice, thyme, rosemary, soy sauce, salt and pepper to a blender along with the red pepper flakes and whizz until smooth.
3. Add in the olive oil to bring the mixture together.
4. Add this garlic rub all over the pork and massage it.
5. Place the pork in the fridge for 8 to 12 hours.
6. Open the lid of the grill and allow a fire to establish.
7. Set the temperature to 400 F and close the lid for 10 minutes.
8. Place the tenderloin on the grill grate and roast for 15 to 20 minutes.
9. Turn the tenderloins around every few minutes until the internal temperature reaches 145 F. If you want it to be well done then wait for the internal temperature to reach 160 F.
10. Allow it to cool down for 5 minutes before carving and serving.

Roast Pork with Mango Salsa

Ingredients:

- 6 pounds pork loin, boneless
- 1 teaspoon chili powder
- 1 tablespoon garlic cloves, chopped
- 1 large onion, chopped
- 1 teaspoon smoked paprika
- 1 teaspoon cayenne pepper
- Salt to taste
- Pepper to taste

For salsa

- 1 pineapple, chopped
- 1 mango, chopped
- 1 cup strawberries, chopped
- 1 tablespoon cilantro leaves, chopped
- Salt to taste
- Pepper to taste
- 1 teaspoon garlic powder
- 1 teaspoon onion powder

Instructions:

1. Place the pork on a plate and sprinkle it with the rub and rub until settled in.
2. Add the pineapple, mango, strawberries, cilantro leaves, and salt, pepper, garlic and onion powder to a bowl and mix until well combined.
3. Open the grill, start the smoker and allow a fire to establish.
4. Set the temperature to 450 F and close the lid for 10 minutes.
5. Add the pork to the grill and turn it around every few minutes.
6. Reduce the heat to 350 F and close the lid for 10 minutes.
7. The internal temperature of the meat should reach 150 F.
8. Remove it from the grill and add to a cutting board.
9. Allow it to cool for 10 minutes before cutting and serving.

Roasted Ham Glaze

Ingredients:

- 10 pounds spiral cut ham, cooked
- 10 to 12 cloves
- 10 to 12 cherries
- 1 large pineapple

For glaze

- 1 cup pineapple juice
- ½ cup brown sugar
- 1 cinnamon stick
- 4 to 5 cloves

Instructions:

1. Open the grill, start the smoker and allow a fire to establish.
2. Set the temperature to 325 f and close the lid for 10 minutes.
3. Rinse the ham and pat it dry to remove excess water.
4. Add the pineapple juice, sugar, cinnamon and cloves to a pan and bring to a boil.
5. Lower the heat and simmer the sauce for 10 minutes it until the sauce thickens.
6. Baste the ham with half of this thickened sauce and cover it fully.
7. Pierce the cloves into the ham and sprinkle the chopped cherries on top.
8. Place the ham in a pan with the fat side up.
9. Place the pan on the grill and cook for about 2 hours.
10. Brush the remaining glaze over the ham and grill for a further 20 minutes.
11. The internal temperature should reach about 160 F.
12. Allow the ham to rest for some time before cutting and serving.

WOOD PELLET SMOKER AND GRILL COOKBOOK

Pork Beer Beans

Ingredients:

- 1 pound bacon
- 3 cups cooked sausage links
- 2 cups pinto beans
- 2 red bell peppers
- 1 large onion, chopped
- 2 garlic cloves, chopped
- 1 onion, chopped
- 1 teaspoon smoked paprika
- 1 teaspoon cumin powder
- Salt to taste
- Pepper to taste
- 1 teaspoon chili powder
- 1 tablespoon Worcestershire sauce
- 1 tablespoon mustard
- ¼ cup brown sugar
- 1 large dried chipotle pepper
- 1 cup apple juice
- 25 ounces beer

Instructions:

1. Open the grill, start the smoker and allow a fire to establish.
2. Set the temperature to 450 f and close the lid for 10 minutes.
3. Add a Dutch oven to the grill and close the lid for 10 minutes.
4. Add the chopped bacon and cook it until crispy brown.
5. Add the bell pepper, onions, sausage and bacon and mix until combined.
6. Grab a bowl. Add in the smoked paprika, garlic cloves, onion, cumin powder, black pepper, salt, chili powder, Worcestershire sauce, yellow mustard, sugar, paprika beans, apple juice, chipotle pepper and mix until well combined.
7. Add all of it to the Dutch oven.
8. Leave it uncovered for 10 minutes and then reduce the heat to 275 F.
9. Cover and cook for 3 hours or until the sauce thicken.
10. Serve hot.

Smoked Bologna

Ingredients:

- 1 pound bologna log
- ¼ cup brown sugar
- 1 tablespoon mustard
- 1 teaspoon soya sauce
- 1 tablespoon Worcestershire sauce

Instructions:

1. Open the lid of the grill and allow a fire to establish.
2. Set the temperature to 450 F and close the lid for 10 minutes.
3. Make small incisions over the bologna using a sharp knife.
4. Add the sugar, mustard, soya sauce and Worcestershire sauce in a bowl and pour over the ham.
5. Reduce the temperature to 230 F and add the bologna for 4 hours.
6. Slice the ham and serve.

Pork Pizza

Ingredients:

- ½ cup pizza sauce
- 2 garlic cloves, chopped
- 10 slices pepperoni
- 2 slices bacon
- 1 sausage link, chopped
- ½ cup beef mince
- Parmesan to sprinkle
- Pepper to sprinkle

Instructions:

1. Open the lid of the grill and allow a fire to establish.
2. Set the temperature to 475 f and close the lid for 10 minutes.
3. Add a cast iron pan to the grill and pour the oil.
4. Add the pizza base to it.
5. Spread the sauce on top.
6. Place the bacon and pepperoni slices on top.
7. Sprinkle with the mozzarella cheese.
8. Place the pizza on the grill and bake for 15 minutes or until the cheese melts.
9. Sprinkle with chili flakes and serve.

Pork Pho

Ingredients:

For brine

- 3 cups water
- Pepper to taste
- ⅔ cups Salt
- ⅔ cups brown sugar
- 5 cups ice

For pho

- Large pork tenderloin
- 2 packs Ramen noodles
- 1 Ramen flavor pack
- 2 tablespoons sugar
- 2 teaspoon fish sauce
- Pepper to taste
- Pepper flakes

To sprinkle

- Lime
- Cilantro
- Beans

Instructions:

1. To make the brine, add the water, salt, sugar, pepper, garlic, and dried thyme and bring to a boil.
2. Once everything dissolves, remove it from the heat and add in the ice.
3. Add the tenderloin to the brine and add to the fridge.
4. Allow the pork to remain there for 5 to 6 hours.
5. Open the grill, start the smoker and allow a fire to establish.
6. Set the temperature to 400 F for 10 minutes.
7. Add the pork to the grill and cook through.

8. Meanwhile, make the pho by boiling 3 cups of water and adding the ramen.
9. Add in the ramen seasoning and mix until well combined.
10. Add in the sugar, fish sauce, pepper flakes and mix well.
11. Add it to a bowl along with the pork.
12. Serve with a sprinkling of lime, cilantro, and beans.

Pork with Mustard and Peach Relish

Ingredients:

- 4 pork chops
- ½ cup basil leaves
- 1 bottle Pork and poultry rub
- ½ cup mustard
- 3 fresh peaches, chopped
- ½ cup blueberries
- 1 large shallot, chopped
- 3 tablespoon olive oil
- 1 teaspoon cardamom powder
- 2 teaspoon honey
- Salt to taste
- Pepper to taste

Instructions:

1. Add the pork and poultry rub over the pork chops.
2. Add the blueberries and peaches to a pan along with the shallots, basil. Vinegar, olive oil, cardamom and honey and mix until combined.
3. Add in salt and pepper and mix well.
4. Baste the pork with this glaze and follow up with mustard.
5. Open the grill, start the smoker and allow a fire to establish.
6. Set the temperature to 450 F and close the lid for 10 minutes.
7. Add the pork to the grill and cook for 10 minutes.
8. The internal temperature should reach 145 F.
9. Add the chops to a plate slice and serve.

Pork and Pepper Skewers

Ingredients:

- 12 ounces sausage, chopped
- 12 ounces tomatoes, chopped
- 1 cup red bell peppers, chopped
- 1 cup yellow bell peppers, chopped
- 1 red onion, chopped
- Olive oil

For ketchup

- ½ cup tomatoes, minced
- ½ tablespoon chipotle
- Pepper to taste
- 1 teaspoon honey
- 1 teaspoon garlic, chopped
- 1 teaspoon onion powder
- ¼ anchovy chili powder

Instructions:

1. Open the grill, start the smoker and allow a fire to establish.
2. Set the temperature to 450 F and close the lid.
3. Chop the onions, pepper, and sausages and insert them through a skewer alternating between them.
4. Drizzle oil over the vegetables and sprinkle with the seasoning.
5. Place the skewers on the grill and flip every few minutes and grill on all sides.
6. To make the sauce, add the tomatoes, chipotle, pepper, honey, garlic, onion, and anchovy chili and mix well.
7. Remove the pork and peppers from the skewer and add to a plate.
8. Drizzle with the sauce and serve.

St. Louis Ribs

Ingredients:

1. 2 racks ribs, bone in
2. 6 ounces game rub
3. 8 ounces apple juice
4. 1 bottle BBQ sauce

Instructions:

1. Remove the membrane from the ribs and apply the rub on the front and the back of the ribs.
2. Allow it to stay for 20 to 30 minutes.
3. Open the grill and start the smoker to establish a fire.
4. Preheat the temperature to 225 F and close the lid for 10 minutes.
5. Place the grills on the grate and cook for an hour.
6. Open the lid and sprinkle some apple juice over it.
7. Cook for 4 hours.
8. The internal temperature should reach 200 F.
9. Once done, brush the ribs with the sauce and grill for a further 10 minutes.
10. Allow it to cool down before cutting and serving.

Kung Pao Pork

Ingredients:

- 12 ounces bacon
- 6 scallions, chopped
- 2 garlic cloves, chopped
- ¼ inch ginger, grated
- 1 red bell pepper, chopped
- 1/4 cup peanuts, roasted

For sauce

- 1 tablespoon Chinese vinegar
- 1 tablespoon soya sauce
- 1 teaspoon hoisin sauce
- 1 teaspoon sesame oil
- 2 teaspoons sugar
- 1 teaspoon cornstarch
- 1 teaspoon Sichuan pepper

Instructions:

1. To make the sauce, add the vinegar, soya sauce, hoisin sauce, sesame oil, sugar, cornstarch and Sichuan pepper.
2. Open the grill and start the smoker to establish a fire.
3. Set the temperature to 375 f and close the lid for 10 minutes.
4. Add the garlic, ginger, scallions, and oil to a pouch and set aside.
5. Once the grill preheats, add the bell pepper and the prepared foil to the grill.
6. Cook for 10 to 12 minutes and turn the packet every few minutes.
7. Cut the pepper and bacon and set aside.
8. Add a skillet to the grill and the scallions, garlic, ginger, bell pepper and stir-fry for a minute.
9. Add in the sauce to coat the vegetables.
10. Add in the peanuts and mix until well combined.
11. Transfer it to a plate, sprinkle with the scallions and serve.

Chapter 7: Seafood Recipes Using a Wood Pellet-Smoker Grill

Smoked Tuna

Ingredients:

- 8 ounces tuna fillets
- 1 cup salt
- 1 cup sugar
- 1 orange, zested
- 1 lemon, zested

Instructions:

1. Add the salt, sugar, lemon zest, orange zest to a bowl and mix until well combined.
2. Leave it on to form brine.
3. Add the filets one each to the brine and make sure they are apart and each tuna is fully covered in brine.
4. Place in the fridge for 5 to 6 hours.
5. Switch on the grill and allow a fire to establish.
6. Set the temperature to 200 F and close the lid for 10 minutes.
7. Remove the fillets out and allow to rest for 40 minutes.
8. Increase the temperature to 225 F and cook for an hour.
9. Remove and serve hot.

Lobster with Garlic Butter

Ingredients:

- 2 pounds cooked lobsters
- 2 tablespoons oil
- 2 lemons, chopped
- Parsley leaves to serve

For Garlic butter

- ¾ cup butter
- 2 tablespoons flat leaf parsley
- 1 tablespoon shallot, chopped
- 2 garlic cloves, chopped
- 1 tablespoon lemon zest
- 1 tablespoon lemon juice
- Salt to taste
- Pepper to taste

Instructions:

1. To make the garlic butter, add the butter to a pan and wait for it to melt.
2. Toss in the shallots and sauté until translucent.
3. Add the garlic, lemon zest, lemon juice salt and pepper and mix until combined.
4. Cut open the cooked lobster and remove the tomalley.
5. Use a brush to apply olive oil all over the lobster.
6. Open the smoker and allow a fire to establish.
7. Set the temperature to 400 F and close the lid for 10 minutes.
8. Once it heats, add the lobster's flesh down on the grill.
9. Add the garlic butter all over the lobster and close the lid again.
10. Cook for 5 minutes.
11. Add to a plate along with the lemon wedges and serve warm.

Halibut with Pesto

Ingredients:

- 5 ounces halibut fillets
- 5 tablespoons canola oil
- Salt to taste
- Pepper to taste
- 1 cup green garlic, chopped
- ⅔ cup parmesan cheese
- ⅓ cup pine nuts
- ⅔ cup olive oil

Instructions:

1. Open the grill and allow a fire to establish.
2. Set the temperature to 500 F and close the lid for 10 minutes.
3. Add a cast iron griddle to the grill.
4. While that heats up add the Parmesan, garlic, pine nuts and pulse until smooth.
5. Add in the olive oil, salt and pepper and whizz until combined.
6. Add oil to the griddle and add in the fish fillets.
7. Close the lid and cook the fish for 4 minutes on both sides.
8. Remove from pan and add to a plate with the garlic butter on top.

Smoked Shrimp

Ingredients:

- ¼ cup olive oil
- ¼ cup lemon juice
- 2 garlic cloves, chopped
- Pepper to taste
- Salt to taste
- 8 ounces mushrooms, chopped
- 1 large bell pepper, chopped
- 1 onion, chopped
- ¼ cup cilantro, chopped
- 1 cup grits
- 1 cup cheddar cheese

Instructions:

1. Add 4 cups of water to a pan and bring to a boil.
2. Add in salt and wait for it to melt.
3. Add in the grits and stir such that no lump is formed.
4. Add to the grill and toss in the cheddar cheese and stir until mixed well.
5. To a bowl add the olive oil, lemon juice, garlic and pepper and mix until well combined.
6. Add in the shrimp and marinate for 5 minutes.
7. Meanwhile, start the grill and allow a fire to establish.
8. Set the temperature to 400 F and close the lid for 10 minutes.
9. Remove the shrimp from the marinade and add to a skewer alternating between the mushrooms, peppers, and onions.
10. Once the grill heats add the skewers and close the lid for 5 minutes.
11. The shrimps should turn light pink.
12. Once done, add the grits to a plate and add the shrimp, peppers, and onions on top and serve.

Salmon in Bun

Ingredients:

- ¼ cup warm milk
- 2 ¼ teaspoon yeast
- 1 large egg
- 2 cups flour

For dough

- 4 large eggs
- 2 cups flour, unbleached
- 10 to 12 tablespoons butter
- Salt to taste
- ⅓ cup sugar

For salmon

- 3 pounds salmon
- 1 cup quinoa
- 2 cups chicken broth
- 2 tablespoons chives
- 1 teaspoon ginger, grated
- 2 teaspoons butter
- 2 cups mushrooms
- ½ cup wine 1 lemon, juiced and zested
- Salt to taste
- Pepper to taste

Instructions:

1. Add the milk, egg, yeast and 1-cup flour to a bowl and mix until well combined.
2. Sprinkle the rest of the flour over it and set aside for an hour.
3. Once done, add in the salt, sugar, egg and 1-cup flour.
4. Start mixing it or use a mixer to do so.

5. Once everything is well mixed, add in the butter and keep mixing.
6. Once done, add to a bowl and cover with cling film and set aside for 2 hours.
7. Once done, remove film and punch the dough down into the bowl.
8. Cover again and let it rise for 4 to 6 hours.
9. Switch on the grill and allow a fire to establish.
10. Set the temperature to 400 F and close the lid for 10 minutes.
11. Add the salmon to a bowl along with the salt and pepper and add to the grill.
12. Meanwhile, add a pan to the grill along with water, oil, and garlic.
13. Once it boils add in the quinoa.
14. Once done, remove and add a pan to the grill along with butter, ginger, and mushrooms and wait for it to sauté.
15. Add in half the white wine, chives and lemon zest and cover.
16. Add the dough on a board and place the quinoa in the center.
17. Add the salmon and mushrooms over it and insert the salmon in between.
18. Add the egg to a bowl along with the water and brush it over the bun.
19. Place on the grill and bake for an hour.
20. Slice and serve hot.

Trout with Butter

Ingredients:

- 1 full rainbow trout
- 1 orange, sliced in circles
- 1 lemon, sliced in circles
- 3 bay leaves
- 4 thyme sprigs
- 1 whole garlic, chopped
- Salt to taste
- 1 teaspoon chipotle pepper, chopped
- 4 tablespoons butter

Instructions:

1. Open the smoker grill and allow a fire to establish.
2. Set the temperature to 400 F and wait for 10 minutes.
3. Add butter to a pan and once it melts add in the lemon.
4. Add the fish to the foil and drizzle the lemon butter on top.
5. Sprinkle with salt and pepper.
6. Sprinkle the bay leaves, thyme, garlic cloves, chipotle, orange and lemon slices and close the packet.
7. Place it on the grill for 15 minutes or until the internal temperature reaches 145 F.
8. Serve warm.

Salmon Tacos

Ingredients:

- 2 pounds salmon fillets
- Salt to taste
- Pepper to taste
- 1 tablespoon ancho chili powder
- 1 tablespoon smoked paprika
- 1 tablespoon brown sugar
- 1 tablespoon garlic, chopped
- ¼ tablespoon oregano
- Olive oil

For salsa

- 1 pound ripe tomatoes
- 1 jalapeno. Chopped
- 1 red onion, chopped
- ½ bunch cilantro leaves, chopped
- Pepper to taste
- Salt to taste
- Olive oil

To top

- Tortillas
- Cabbage, shredded
- Limes
- Cilantro to sprinkle

Instructions:

1. Add the salt, ancho chili, paprika, brown sugar, garlic, oregano, and pepper to a bowl and mix until well combined.
2. Open the grill and allow a fire to establish.
3. Set the temperature to 275 F and close the lid for 10 minutes.

4. Make a small incision in the tomatoes and add to the grill along with the onions, jalapenos and brush some oil on top.
5. Add to the grill and close lid for 30 minutes to give them a smoky flavor.
6. For the cabbage, add it to a bowl and squeeze lemon on top.
7. Sprinkle with salt and pepper and add to fridge until ready to serve.
8. Raise the grill temperature to 400 f and close the lid for 10 minutes.
9. Add the salmon and cook for 20 minutes or until the internal temperature reaches 125 F.
10. Add to a plate and allow it to rest for 10 minutes.
11. Serve with the tacos, lime juice, cilantro, salsa, and cabbage salad on top.

Fish Chowder

Ingredients:

- 10 ounces salmon fillet
- Salmon shake
- 2 corn ears
- 3 strips bacon
- 4 cans potato soup
- 4 cans whole milk
- 8 ounces cream cheese
- 3 cups scallions, chopped
- 2 teaspoons hot sauce

Instructions:

1. Start the grill and allow a fire to establish.
2. Raise the temperature to 350 F and close the lid for 10 minutes.
3. Add the salmon to the grill and cook for 30 minutes.
4. Add to a plate and pull using a fork.
5. Add the corn and bacon to the grill and close lid for 10 minutes.
6. Grill for 15 minutes or until they develop spots.
7. Meanwhile, add the potato soup and milk to a pan and bring to a boil.
8. Add in the cream cheese and whisk until well combined.
9. Cut the cob and bacon into long strips.
10. Add the green onion to the soup along with the salmon and mix well.
11. Heat for 10 minutes.
12. Serve hot.

Smoked Scallops

Ingredients:

- 10 scallops
- 10 bacon slices
- 1 tablespoon butter
- Salt to taste
- Pepper to taste
- Toothpicks

Instructions:

1. Switch on the smoker and allow a fire to establish.
2. Set the temperature to 325 F and close the lid for 10 minutes.
3. Wrap the bacon slices around the scallops and use a toothpick to secure it in place.
4. Brush the butter over it and sprinkle with salt and pepper.
5. Add to the grill and close lid for 10 minutes.
6. Once done, allow to cool for 10 minutes.
7. Serve with a drizzle of melted butter on top.

Chapter 8: Extras Using a Wood Pellet-Smoker Grill

Salmon Candy

Ingredients:

- 5 pounds salmon fillets
- 1 pound sugar
- 1 cup maple syrup
- 1 cup salt

Instructions:

1. Add the salt and sugar to a bowl and mix until well combined.
2. Remove half of it out and flatten the mixture.
3. Place the salmon skin side down and cover with the rest of the sugar and salt.
4. Cover it and place in the fridge for an hour.
5. Once done, remove and place the fish under running water to clean it.
6. Allow it to dry for 2 hours.
7. Switch on the grill and allow a fire to establish.
8. Preheat to 180 F and close the lid for 10 minutes.
9. Add it to the grill and grill for 4 hours.
10. Open the lid every 2 hours to add a little maple syrup on top.
11. Add more about 10 minutes before switching off.
12. Allow it to cool down before adding to the fridge.
13. Cut and serve.

Smoked Popcorn

Ingredients:

- 5 tablespoons butter
- 2 tablespoon oil
- 2 teaspoon seasoning
- 1 teaspoon garlic, chopped
- Salt to taste
- ¼ cup pop kernels
- ½ cup parmesan cheese
- 1 lunch bag

Instructions:

1. Start the smoker and allow a fire to establish.
2. Set the temperature to 250 F and close the lid for 10 minutes.
3. Add a pan to the grill and add the butter, garlic, salt, pepper, and seasoning and set aside.
4. Add the kernels to a bag and microwave it for 2 minutes.
5. Once done, add to a bowl along with the butter mixture and toss.
6. Add to a baking sheet and place over the grill for 10 minutes.
7. Serve hot.

Pepper Beef Jerky

Ingredients:

- 1 can dark beer
- 1 cup soy sauce
- ¼ cup Worcestershire sauce
- 3 tablespoons brown sugar
- Salt to taste
- 1 teaspoon garlic, chopped
- Pepper to taste
- 2 pounds trimmed beef

Instructions:

1. Add the beer, soya sauce, Worcestershire sauce, brown sugar, salt, garlic and pepper to a bowl and mix until well combined.
2. Using a sharp knife, slice the beef against the grain.
3. Remove any tissue and fat from the meat.
4. Add the beef to a bag and pour the sauce mixture over it and shake until well combined.
5. Add the bag to the fridge.
6. Open the grill and allow a fire to establish.
7. Set the temperature to 450 F and close the lid for 10 minutes.
8. Remove the beef and discard the marinade.
9. Dry the beef.
10. Sprinkle the salt and pepper on the beef.
11. Add it to the grill and smoke for 5 hours.
12. Add to a board when the beef is warm.
13. Slice and serve.

Granola Bars

Ingredients:

- 3 cups oats
- ¼ cups coconut
- ½ cup almonds, chopped
- ⅓ cup honey
- ¼ cup sugar
- ¼ cup butter
- 1 teaspoon vanilla
- 1 teaspoon chia seeds
- Salt to taste
- ¼ cup cranberries, chopped
- ¼ cup apricots, chopped

Instructions:

1. Open the grill and allow a fire to establish.
2. Set the temperature to 350 F and close the lid for 10 minutes.
3. Add parchment paper to a baking tray and spray with cooking spray.
4. On another tray mix the coconut, oats, and almonds.
5. Add it to a bowl along with the cranberries and apricots and mix until well combined.
6. Add the butter, honey, chia seeds, sugar, vanilla and salt to a pan and mix until well combined.
7. Pour this all over the nuts and fruits.
8. Allow it to cool for 10 minutes.
9. Transfer it to a parchment paper and use a spatula to spread around.
10. Add to the fridge for 2 hours or until it hardens.
11. Cut and serve.

Smoke Roasted Olives

Ingredients:

- 2 cups black and green olives
- 3 rosemary sprigs
- 2 garlic cloves, chopped
- 2 teaspoons orange zest, grated
- 2 tablespoons red chili flakes
- ⅓ cup olive oil
- 2 tablespoons orange juice

Instructions:

1. Add the rosemary, garlic, orange zest, red chili flakes, olive oil and orange juice to a pan and cover with foil.
2. Turn on the grill and wait for a fire to establish.
3. Set the temperature to 300 F and close the lid.
4. Add the olives to the grill and roast for 45 minutes.
5. Serve as an extra.

Stuffed Jalapenos

Ingredients:

- 40 jalapeno peppers
- 8 ounces cream cheese
- 1 cup cheddar cheese
- 2 teaspoons pork shake
- 2 tablespoons sour cream
- 1 pack sausages
- 20 slices bacon

Instructions:

1. Cut the tops of the jalapenos and use a knife or spoon to scoop out the inner membrane and seeds.
2. Add the cream cheese, grated cheese, pork rub and sour cream to a bowl and mix until well combined.
3. Add this to a piping bag.
4. Stuff the jalapenos with this mixture right to the top.
5. Wrap the jalapenos with the bacon slices and use a toothpick to secure.
6. Open the grill and allow a fire to establish.
7. Set the temperature to 350 F and close the lid for 10 minutes.
8. Add the jalapenos and cook for 30 minutes.
9. Serve hot.

Smoked Eggs

Ingredients:

- ½ cup all-purpose flour
- 4 teaspoons pork rub
- 4 hard-boiled eggs
- 1 pound seasoned sausage
- 1 raw egg, beaten
- 1 cup bread crumbs
- 1 cup mayonnaise
- ¼ cup Dijon mustard
- Lettuce leaves
- Pickles

Instructions:

1. Add the flour and pork rub to a bowl and mix until well combined.
2. Dip the boiled eggs in the water and roll over the flour to coat fully.
3. Cut the sausage into 4 parts and flatten down using your palm.
4. Wrap the egg with the sausage and cover on all sides.
5. Dip it in the egg mixture and shake to remove excess.
6. Roll it into the breadcrumbs.
7. Add the eggs to the fridge for 2 hours.
8. Turn on the grill and allow a fire to establish.
9. Raise the temperature to 375 F and close the lid for 10 minutes.
10. Add it to the grill and grill for 30 minutes.
11. Use a sharp knife to cut the eggs into quarters.
12. Add the mustard, mayonnaise and pork rub to a bowl and mix until well combined.
13. Drizzle this over the eggs and serve.

Crab Dip

Ingredients:

- ⅓ cup mayonnaise
- 3 ounces sour cream
- 1 teaspoon paprika powder
- ¼ teaspoon cayenne powder
- 2 cups crab meat
- 3 scallions, chopped
- Salt to taste
- Pepper to taste
- Butter crackers
- Scallions, chopped

Instructions:

1. Open the grill and allow a fire to establish.
2. Set the temperature at 350 F and close the lid for 10 minutes.
3. In the meantime, add the mayonnaise, sour cream, paprika powder, cayenne powder, crabmeat, scallions, salt, and pepper to a bowl and mix until well combined.
4. Add it to a baking dish and add to the grill.
5. Bake for 30 minutes or until bubbly and golden.
6. Sprinkle with the scallions and crackers and serve.

Smoked Cheese

Ingredients:

- 8 ounces cream cheese
- 1 tablespoon Worcestershire sauce
- 1 teaspoon hot sauce
- 3 cups cheddar cheese
- 8 bacon slices
- 2 onions, chopped
- 1 cup pecans, chopped

Instructions:

1. Add the cream and cheddar cheese to a bowl and mix until well combined.
2. Add in the Worcestershire and hot sauce and mix well.
3. Add in the crumbled bacon and onions and mix until combined.
4. Cover it with film and place in the fridge for 4 hours.
5. Once it's firm, shape it into a log.
6. Wrap it tightly with cling film.
7. Add to the fridge overnight.
8. Open the grill and allow a fire to establish.
9. Remove the lid and add to the grill for an hour.
10. Once done, add to a plate and serve hot.

Scallion Muffins

Ingredients:

- 1 cup all-purpose flour
- 1 cup cornmeal
- ¼ cup sugar
- 1 teaspoon baking powder
- 1 teaspoon baking soda
- Salt to taste
- Pepper to taste
- 1 teaspoon paprika powder
- 2 cups corn
- 4 scallions, chopped
- 5 bacon, chopped
- 2 eggs
- 1 cup sour cream
- 5 tablespoons butter

Instructions:

1. Open the grill and allow a fire to establish.
2. Set the temperature to 350 f and close the lid for 10 minutes.
3. To a bowl add the flour, cornmeal, sugar, baking powder, baking soda, salt, pepper and cayenne and mix until well combined.
4. Add the corn, scallions, and bacon and mix well.
5. Add eggs, cream, and butter to another bowl and whisk until well combined.
6. Mix the two together until well combined.
7. Pour it out into muffin tins and fill half way up.
8. Add them to the grill for 30 minutes or until they rise fully.
9. Serve hot.

Smoked Corn Salsa

Ingredients:

- 4 large corn ears
- 4 tomatoes, chopped
- ½ cup cilantro, chopped
- 1 onion, chopped
- 1 teaspoon garlic powder
- 1 teaspoon onion powder
- 1 jalapeno, chopped
- 1 lime, chopped
- Salt to taste
- Pepper to taste

Instructions:

1. Open the grill and allow a fire to establish.
2. Set the temperature to 450 F and close the lid.
3. Add the corn to the grill and grill until it chars.
4. Meanwhile, add the tomatoes, cilantro, onion, garlic powder, onion powder, jalapeno, lime, salt, and pepper to a bowl and mix until well combined.
5. Once the corn is done, add it to the salsa and mix well.
6. Serve as a side.

Chapter 9: Brines Using a Wood Pellet-Smoker Grill
Brined Turkey

Ingredients:

- 10 pounds turkey
- 5 quarts hot water
- 3 cups salt
- 1 cup maple syrup
- ½ cup brown sugar
- 1 large onion, peeled and chopped
- 4 orange strips, chopped
- 3 whole bay leaves
- Pepper to taste
- 1 tablespoon cloves
- 3 quarts ice
- 1 cup butter, melted
- Pork rub
- Thyme, rosemary sprigs
- Cilantro leaves to sprinkle

Instructions:

1. Add the water, salt, sugar, bourbon, maple syrup, onions, bay leaves, orange peels, pepper, and cloves to a pot and bring to a boil.
2. Add in the ice and mix well.
3. Rinse the turkey thoroughly.
4. Add it to the brine and add to the fridge for 12 hours.
5. Once done, remove and pat dry.
6. Use a sharp knife to cut off the wings and tails.
7. Add the remaining butter and maple syrup to a bowl and mix until well combined.
8. Add the salt, pork shake, pepper and mix well.
9. Open the grill and allow a fire to establish.
10. Set the temperature to 350 F and close the lid for 10 minutes.
11. Add the turkey and roast it for 3 hours.

12. The internal temperature should reach 165 F.
13. Brush it with the butter and maple syrup.
14. Allow the turkey to rest for 20 minutes.
15. Slice and serve with a sprinkling of cilantro on top.

Brined Beef Pastrami

Ingredients:

- 6 quarts water
- 2 cups salt
- 1 cup sugar
- ⅔ cup brown sugar
- Salt to taste
- 1 tablespoon pickling spices
- 1 teaspoon mustard paste
- 10 garlic cloves, chopped
- 1 teaspoon mustard seeds
- 7 pounds beef brisket
- ¼ cup peppercorns
- 2 tablespoons coriander seeds

Instructions:

1. Add the water, salt, sugar, pepper, pickling spices, mustard seeds and garlic to a pot and bring to a boil.
2. Add in the salt and sugar and mix until dissolved.
3. Add it to the fridge and allow it to chill.
4. Use a sharp knife to poke holes over the beef.
5. Add the brine to a pan and immerse the brisket.
6. Cover with cling film and let it rest for 5 to 6 days.
7. Once done, remove and pat it dry.
8. Place it on a rack for 24 hours.
9. Open the grill and allow a fire to establish.
10. Set the temperature to 225 f and close the lid for 10 minutes.
11. Add the beef to the grill and grill for 4 hours.
12. Remove from grill and add to a plastic bag and let it rest for some time.
13. Slice and serve.

Smoked Cucumber Pickles

Ingredients:

- 1 pound cucumbers
- 1 cup salt
- ½ cup sugar
- 5 garlic cloves
- 5 bay leaves
- Pepper to taste
- 2 tablespoons white pepper
- 5 tablespoons fennel seeds
- 1 tablespoon whole coriander seeds
- 1 tablespoon red pepper flakes
- 1 bunch dill leaves
- 2 cups vinegar
- 2 cups ice

Instructions:

1. Open the grill and allow a fire to establish.
2. Set the temperature to 350 f and close the lid for 10 minutes.
3. Add the whole cucumbers to the grill and grill for 45 minutes.
4. Remove from the grill and cut into shapes of your choice.
5. To make the brine add the salt, sugar, garlic, cloves, bay leaves, white pepper, fennel seeds, coriander seeds, pepper flakes, dill leaves, vinegar to a pan and bring to a boil.
6. Simmer it for 10 minutes.
7. Once done, add ice cubes to cool it down.
8. Once cool, pour it over the cucumbers.
9. Allow it to stay for 24 hours.
10. Serve as a side.

Brined Pork Chops

Ingredients:

- 2 quarts water
- ⅓ cup salt
- ¼ cup sugar
- 1 onion, chopped
- 8 ounces pork, bone in
- Pepper to taste

For toppings

- 2 lemons, cut lengthwise
- ½ orange
- 1 shallot, chopped
- ¼ cup rice wine vinegar
- 2 tablespoons honey
- Salt to taste
- Pepper to taste
- ¾ cup olive oil
- Parsley to sprinkle

Instructions:

1. Add the water, salt, and sugar to a large container and mix until well combined.
2. Add in the onions and pork chops and mix well.
3. Cover and place in the fridge for 8 hours.
4. Switch on the grill and allow a fire to establish.
5. Raise the temperature to 450 F and close the lid for 10 minutes.
6. Drain the excess brine and pat the pork dry.
7. Sprinkle with salt and pepper and add to the grill.
8. Close and grill for 15 minutes.
9. The internal temperature should reach 145 F.
10. In the meantime add the lemon and orange rind to a bowl along with the shallots, vinegar, honey, salt and pepper and mix well. Add the pork to a plate and drizzle the vinaigrette on top.
11. Serve warm.

Apple Mustard Pork Loin

Ingredients:

- ¾ cup salt
- ¾ cup sugar
- 1-quart water
- 1-quart apple juice
- 3 garlic cloves, chopped
- 2 bay leaves
- 5-pound pork loin
- Pepper to taste
- Salt to taste
- 2 cups apple cider
- 1 tablespoon rosemary, chopped
- 3 tablespoon mustard
- 1 tablespoon honey
- 1 tablespoon apple liqueur
- 2 teaspoons molasses

Instructions:

1. Add the salt, sugar, water, brine, garlic and bay leaves to a pot and stir until well combined.
2. Add the roast to a bag and add in the brine.
3. Seal and keep in the fridge overnight.
4. Remove and pat it dry.
5. Place it in a roasting pan and season with salt and pepper.
6. Switch on the grill and allow a fire to establish.
7. Set the temperature at 350 F and close the lid for 10 minutes.
8. To make the glaze add the cider, rosemary, to a pan and bring to a boil until it thickens.
9. Add the mustard, honey, apple liqueur and molasses to the pan and whisk until combined.
10. Add the pork to the grill and roast for an hour.
11. The internal temperature should reach 145 F.
12. Allow it to rest for 10 minutes.
13. Add to a plate, slice and serve with a drizzle of the glaze on top.

Chinese Chicken Breast

Ingredients:

- 2 quarts water
- ½ cup salt
- ¼ cup brown sugar
- ½ cup soya sauce
- 8 ounces chicken breast
- 2 tablespoons garlic, chopped
- Scallions to sprinkle

Instructions:

1. Add the water, salt, soya sauce to a pan and bring to a boil.
2. Immerse the chicken in it and place in the fridge for 2 hours.
3. Remove and pat using a towel.
4. Open the grill and allow a fire to establish.
5. Set the temperature to 350 f and close the lid for 10 minutes.
6. Add the chicken to the grill and roast for 30 minutes.
7. Add a pan to the grill and toss in the garlic and roast till brown.
8. Add the chicken to a plate, slice and serve with a sprinkling of the scallions and garlic on top.

Cheese Canapés

Ingredients:

- 1 duck breast
- 1 teaspoon game rub
- 1 large sheet puff pastry
- 9 ounces goat's cheese, sliced
- 1 teaspoon thyme leaves
- Arugula
- 2 teaspoons chives, chopped
- Olive oil

Instructions:

1. Add the duck to salt water and let it soak overnight.
2. Switch on the grill and allow a fire to establish.
3. Set the temperature to 165 F and close the lid.
4. Add the duck to a plate and pat it dry.
5. Season it with the game rub and place on the grill for 30 minutes.
6. Increase the temperature to 350 F.
7. Use a cookie cutter to cut out circles from the puff pastry.
8. Add them to the grill and bake for 5 minutes or until they puff up.
9. Add a piece of cheese over each pastry base.
10. Pull the duck using a fork and sprinkle it over the canapés.
11. Sprinkle the thyme leaves along with the chives and drizzle the oil.
12. Place the lettuce and arugula on a plate and transfer the canapés over it.
13. Serve warm.

WOOD PELLET SMOKER AND GRILL COOKBOOK

Brined Fish Salad

Ingredients:

- ½ cup salt
- ⅓ cup sugar
- 2 quarts water
- 2 cups vodka
- 1 whole white fish

For salad

- ½ cup celery, chopped
- ½ cup onion, chopped
- 2 tablespoon lemon juice
- 2 tablespoons dill leaves
- ¾ cup mayonnaise
- ¼ cup sour cream
- ½ teaspoon pepper

Instructions:

1. Add the salt, sugar, water, and vodka to a pan and bring to a boil.
2. Add in the fish and cover with cling film.
3. Add to the fridge and let it brine for 8 hours or overnight.
4. Remove to a plate and pat it dry using a paper towel.
5. Switch on the grill and allow a fire to establish.
6. Set the temperature to 350 F and close the lid.
7. Add the fish to the grill grate and smoke for 3 hours.
8. The internal temperature should reach 150 F.
9. To make a salad, pull the fish using a fork and add to a bowl.
10. Add in the celery, onion, lemon juice, mayonnaise, dill leaves, sour cream and pepper and mix until well combined.
11. Place lettuce leaves on a plate and serve the fish salad on top.

Pickled Beetroots

Ingredients:

- 5 large beetroots, chopped
- 1 cup white wine
- ½ cup honey
- Salt to taste
- 1 cup water
- 9 whole cloves
- Pepper to taste
- 2-star anise
- 1 cinnamon stick, broken in half

Instructions:

- Make a pouch using foil and make a few holes using a fork.
- Add in the beetroots and make a tight packet.
- Open the grill and allow a fire to establish.
- Set the temperature to 350 F and close the lid for 10 minutes.
- Add the beets to it and roast for an hour.
- Remove the foil and allow the beets to cool down.
- Meanwhile, make the brine by adding the vinegar, sugar, salt, and water to a pan and bring to a boil.
- Add in the cloves, pepper, star anise, and cinnamon and close the lid.
- Remove the skins from the beets and add to a jar.
- Pour the brine over it and refrigerate for 5 days.
- Serve as a side.

Brined Ham with Mustard

Ingredients:

- 10 pounds ham
- ½ cup salt
- ½ cup salt
- ¾ cup sugar
- 2 quarts water
- 2 whole cloves
- 1 tablespoon pork shake
- 2 cups apple juice
- ¼ cup maple syrup
- ¼ cup bourbon
- ¼ cup dry mustard
- ½ cup brown sugar
- Pepper to taste
- 2 cups whipping cream
- 4 yolks, beaten

Instructions:

1. Add the salt, sugar, water and brown sugar to a large pan containing water and bring to a boil.
2. Add in ice cubes to cool it down.
3. Submerge the ham and transfer to a plastic bag.
4. Add the bag to the fridge for 2 days.
5. Rinse the ham and pat it dry.
6. Use a sharp knife to make small incisions over the ham.
7. Insert a clove inside each of the incisions.
8. Sprinkle the pork shake over the ham and rub it in.
9. Open the grill and allow a fire to establish.
10. Set the temperature to 300 F and close the lid for 10 minutes.
11. Add the ham to the grill and cook for 30 to 40 minutes.
12. The internal temperature should reach 165 F.
13. Add the ham to a cutting board and allow it to cool down.
14. Meanwhile, add the mustard, brown sugar, salt, and pepper to a pan and whisk until well combined.
15. Add in the vinegar and mix well.
16. Add in the cream and yolks and mix.
17. Pour this over the ham and serve.

Chapter 10: Rubs Using a Wood Pellet-Smoker Grill

Sriracha Wings

Ingredients:

- 2 tablespoons chicken rub
- 2 tablespoons garlic
- 1 tablespoon sesame oil
- 2 pounds chicken

For sauce

- 5 tablespoons butter
- ⅓ cup sugar
- ¼ cup sriracha
- 2 tablespoons soya sauce
- 2 tablespoons lime zest
- 1 tablespoon garlic, chopped
- 1 tablespoon ginger, chopped
- 1 tablespoon cilantro chopped
- 1 tablespoon sesame seeds, toasted
- 1 tablespoon lemon juice

Instructions:

1. Open the grill and allow a fire to establish.
2. Set the temperature to 325 F and close the lid for 10 minutes.
3. Add the rub, garlic powder, salt, pepper, sesame oil and wings to a bowl and mix until well combined.
4. Add to the grill and cook until the internal temperature reaches 165 F.
5. In the meantime, add the butter, sugar, sriracha, soya sauce, lime zest, garlic, ginger and lemon juice to a bowl and mix until well combined.
6. Remove the chicken from the grill and add to the sauce.
7. Add it back to the grill and grill for 10 minutes or until it caramelizes.
8. Serve with chopped cilantro and sesame seeds.

Brisket Sandwich

Ingredients:

- 10 burger buns
- 8-pound brisket
- Spicy beef rub

For sauce

- ¼ cup mustard
- ½ cup ketchup
- ½ cup barbecue sauce
- ¾ cup mayonnaise
- ¼ cup pickles, chopped

Instructions:

1. Place the brisket on a plate and sprinkle the rub over it.
2. Massage it until it is well coated.
3. Add the salt and pepper on top.
4. Wrap it with cling film and place in the fridge.
5. Open the grill and allow a fire to establish.
6. Set the temperature to 450 F and close the lid for 10 minutes.
7. Add the brisket to the grill grate and cook for 4 hours.
8. Once done, turn the grill up to 450 F.
9. The internal temperature should reach 160 F.
10. Remove the brisket and add to foil.
11. Meanwhile, add the ketchup, barbecue sauce, mayonnaise, and chopped pickles to a bowl and mix until well combined.
12. Remove the brisket out and let it sit for 30 minutes.
13. Apply the mustard mix inside the burger buns.
14. Add a lettuce inside the buns.
15. Slice the brisket and add it to the bun.
16. Serve hot.

Braised Duck Legs

Ingredients:

- 2 onions, halved
- 2 carrots, chopped
- 2 celery ribs, chopped
- 2 garlic cloves, chopped
- 2 bay leaves
- 1 bunch thyme leaves
- 1 rosemary sprig
- 2 cups wine
- 3 quarts chicken stock
- Canola oil
- Salt to taste
- Pepper to taste
- 1 tablespoon brown sugar
- 6 whole duck legs

Instructions:

1. Add the salt, pepper, sugar, and thyme to a bowl and mix until well combined.
2. Add the duck legs to the mix and rub well.
3. Place in fridge overnight.
4. Remove from fridge, wash and pat dry.
5. Open the grill and allow the fire to establish.
6. Set the temperature to 350 F and close the lid for 10 minutes.
7. Add a griddle to the grill.
8. Add the duck legs and roast until crisp before flipping.
9. Add in the garlic, celery, bay leaves, thyme, rosemary leaves, salt, pepper, onions, carrots and wine and mix until well combined.
10. Add in the stock to cover the duck legs fully.
11. Reduce the heat down to 350 F.
12. Cook for 2 hours.
13. Once done, add to foil and wrap tightly.
14. Meanwhile, add the braising liquid to a pan and bring to a boil.
15. Add in the salt and pepper and mix well.
16. Slice the duck and add to a plate along with the braising liquid on top.

Chicken Enchiladas

Ingredients:

- 4 pounds chicken
- 3 tablespoons olive oil
- 1 onion, chopped
- 1 can green chilies
- 1 can beans
- 8 to 10 tortillas
- 3 cups cheese, shredded
- 2 cups enchilada sauce
- Salt to taste
- Pepper to taste
- ¼ cup cilantro leaves

Instructions:

1. Open the grill and allow a fire to establish.
2. Preheat the grill to 350 F and close the lid for 10 minutes.
3. Add the chicken to a bowl and drizzle with the oil.
4. Season with salt and pepper and rub it in.
5. Add the chicken to the grill grate and cook for an hour or until the internal temperature reaches 165 F.
6. To make the tortillas lay the tortillas out on a tray and add the sauce on top.
7. Add the beans and a spoonful of the chicken over it.
8. Roll them up and add to a baking tray.
9. Drizzle the remaining sauce on top of the tortillas.
10. Sprinkle the cheese on top.
11. Add the tray to the grill and grill at 350 F for 10 to 15 minutes.
12. Serve hot.

Pecan Pork Loin

Ingredients:

- 6 pounds pork loin
- 2 onions, chopped
- 2 cups pecan nuts
- 2 cups maple syrup
- ½ cup ketchup
- ½ cup vinegar
- ½ cup lemon juice
- 2 tablespoons olive oil
- 2 tablespoons pork rub
- 1 teaspoon pepper sauce

Instructions:

1. Use a sharp knife to make incisions on the pork loin.
2. Add the butter to a pan and toss in the onions until brown.
3. Add in the pecans, ketchup, maple syrup, vinegar, lemon juice, lemon zest, olive oil, hot pepper sauce and pork rub and mix until well combined.
4. Add in the pork loin and mix well.
5. Add to the fridge overnight.
6. Remove the loin and drain the mixture through a sieve and remove the onions and pecans.
7. Add the pork to a board and sprinkle with salt and pepper.
8. Open the grill and allow a fire to establish.
9. Set the temperature to 275 F and close the lid for 10 minutes.
10. Place the groin on the grill and close the lid.
11. Cook for 20 minutes or until the internal temperature reaches 145 F.
12. Slice and serve.

Beef Sandwich

Ingredients:

- 4 pounds beef roast
- Olive oil
- 5 garlic cloves, chopped
- 1 bottle rib rub
- 2 teaspoon Italian seasoning
- 1 large onion, chopped
- 5 cups beef broth
- 8 hoagie buns
- 2 cups red peppers, chopped and stir fried
- 1 cup pickles of your choice

Instructions:

1. Open the grill and allow a fire to establish.
2. Set the temperature to 300 F and close the lid for 10 minutes.
3. Add the rib rub and Italian seasoning to a pan and mix well.
4. Use a sharp knife to make cuts on the beef.
5. Insert garlic into the cuts.
6. Add the pork to a pan and add in the onions.
7. Pour the beef broth over it.
8. Add to the grill until the internal temperature reaches 145 F.
9. Once done, add it to a foil and pour the sauce over it.
10. Wrap it tightly.
11. Once done, add to a cutting board and cut across the grain.
12. Open the buns and dip them into the sauce.
13. Slice the pork and add to the buns.
14. Add the peppers and pickles and serve warm.

Venison Tacos

Ingredients:

- 1 pound venison steak
- 2 tablespoon game rub
- 4 tortillas
- ¼ cup parmesan cheese
- 1 avocado, chopped
- ¼ cup cilantro leaves

For salsa

- ½ pound tomatoes
- 1 jalapeno
- 2 garlic cloves
- 1 onion, chopped
- 2 limes, juiced
- 3 ancho chilies
- ½ cup cilantro leaves

Instructions:

1. Add the steak to a plate and sprinkle the rub on top.
2. Open the grill and allow a fire to establish.
3. Set the temperature to 350 F and close the lid for 10 minutes.
4. Add the venison to the grill and cook for 30 minutes.
5. Cook until the internal temperature reaches 110 F.
6. Meanwhile, add the tomatoes, jalapeno, garlic, onion, limes, and ancho chilies to a pan and mix well.
7. Once cooked, add to a blender to make a smooth paste.
8. Add the cilantro leaves on top.
9. Add the steaks to the cutting board and drizzle the salsa on top.
10. Serve hot.

Turkey Meatballs

Ingredients:

- 2 pounds ground turkey
- 1 jalapeno pepper, chopped
- ¼ teaspoon chipotle rub
- Salt to taste
- Pepper to taste
- 1 onion, chopped
- 1 tablespoon cayenne pepper
- 1 teaspoon Worcestershire sauce
- ¼ cup milk
- 1 egg, beaten

For glaze

- 1 cup cranberry sauce
- ½ cup marmalade
- ½ cup chicken broth
- 1 tablespoon jalapeno pepper
- Salt to taste
- Pepper to taste

Instructions:

1. Add the milk and breadcrumbs to a bowl and mix well.
2. To another bowl add the turkey, garlic, chipotle rub, onion powder, salt, pepper, Worcestershire sauce, egg and jalapenos and mix until well combined.
3. Add in the breadcrumb mixture and mix until well combined.
4. Cover with film and add to the fridge.
5. Open the grill and allow a fire to establish.
6. Preheat the grill to 350 F and close the lid for 10 minutes.
7. Make small balls out of the turkey and add to parchment paper.
8. Add them to the grill and cook until the internal temperature reaches 175 F.
9. Add the cranberry sauce, marmalade, chicken broth, jalapenos to a pan and mix until well combined.
10. When the meatballs are halfway through, brush them with the sauce.
11. Add to a plate and serve.

Chicken Curry

Ingredients:

- 3 pounds chicken
- 2 tablespoons chicken rub
- 3 onions, chopped
- 2 tablespoons butter
- Salt to taste
- 2 bay leaves
- 1 garlic clove, chopped
- 3 tablespoons curry powder
- 4 cups chicken stock
- 2 tablespoons tomato sauce

For sauce

- 2 tablespoons coconut
- 1 apple, peeled and chopped
- 2 tablespoons cornstarch
- 1 cup cream
- Salt to taste

Instructions:

1. Open the grill and allow a fire to establish.
2. Set the temperature to 350 F and close the lid for 10 minutes.
3. Add the chicken to a bowl along with the oil and rub and mix until combined.
4. Add it to the grill and grill for 30 minutes or until the internal temperature reaches 165 F.
5. Remove from the grill and shred into bitc sized pieces.
6. Add the butter, salt, onions, garlic, bay leaves, thyme, curry powder and tomato sauce and stock and mix until well combined.
7. Add the chicken to a pan and bring to a boil.
8. Cook for 40 minutes or until the chicken tenderizes.
9. To make the sauce, add the coconut, apple, cream, and salt to a pan and bring to a boil.
10. Add in water if it is too thick.
11. Stir in the cornstarch and mix well.
12. Add the chicken to a plate and serve with a drizzle of the sauce on top.

Chapter 11: Conversion Chart

Reference Source: https://www.infoplease.com/science-health/weights-measures/us-metric-cooking-conversions

Measure	Equivalent
1 tbsp. (tbsp.) =	3 tsp. (tsp)
$^1/16$ cup =	1 tablespoon
$^1/8$ cup =	2 tablespoons
$^1/6$ cup =	2 tbsp. + 2 teaspoons
$^1/4$ cup =	4 tablespoons
$^1/3$ cup =	5 tbsp. + 1 teaspoon
$^3/8$ cup =	6 tablespoons
$^1/2$ cup =	8 tablespoons
$^2/3$ cup =	10 tbsp. + 2 teaspoons
$^3/4$ cup =	12 tablespoons
1 cup =	48 teaspoons
1 cup =	16 tablespoons
8 fluid ounces (fly oz.) =	1 cup
1 pint (pt.) =	2 cups
1 quart (qtr.) =	2 pints
4 cups =	1 quart
1 gallon (gal) =	4 quarts
16 ounces (oz) =	1 pound (lb)

Metric to U.S.

Capacity		Weight	
1 milliliter	¹/5 teaspoon	1 gram	.035 ounce
5 ml	1 teaspoon	100 grams	3.5 ounces
15 ml	1 tablespoon	500 grams	1.10 pounds
100 ml	3.4 fluid oz	1 kilogram	2.205 pounds = 35 ounces
240 ml	1 cup		
1 liter	34 fluid oz = 4.2 cups = 2.1 pints = 1.06 quarts = 0.26 gallon		

Conclusion

I thank you once again for choosing this book and hope you had a good time reading it.

The main aim of this book was to introduce you to the world of wood pellet smoker grills.

Once you start using it, you will realize how simple it is to cook and become a fan of the tasty food that it can produce.

So what are you waiting for? Heat up that wood pellet smoker grill and start cooking!

Happy cooking!

Made in the USA
Middletown, DE
07 August 2017